Inhalt

Englisch lernen mit Berlitz®

Stephen KING

The Breathing Method

Berlitz Publishing

München • New York • Singapur

Berlitz Englisch lernen mit Stephen King
The Breathing Method

Vokabelerklärungen und Übungen: Helen Galloway
Lektorat: Gaby Bauer-Negenborn
Layout: Ute Weber
Cover-Gestaltung: Dominik Lommer
Projektleitung: Eva Betz

Berlitz Publishing
Mies-van-der-Rohe-Straße 1
D-80807 München

Satz: Franzis print&media GmbH, München
Druck: CS-Druck CornelsenStürtz, Berlin
Printed in Germany
ISBN 978-3-468-79238-0

1. 2. 3. 4. 5. 12 11 10 09 08

Liebe Leserin, lieber Leser,

mit dem spannenden Kurzroman von Stephen King halten Sie endlich ein Englischbuch in der Hand, das Sie garantiert nicht mehr weglegen wollen. Und vor lauter Nervenkitzel merken Sie vielleicht gar nicht, dass Sie ganz nebenbei auch Ihre Englischkenntnisse gehörig auffrischen und erweitern.
Damit Ihr Lesevergnügen nicht durch das Nachschlagen unbekannter Wörter gemindert wird, sind die schwierigsten Vokabeln im Text blau markiert und in der Marginalspalte übersetzt. Interessante Wörter, die in einer Infobox erklärt werden, sind zusätzlich mit einem Sternchen gekennzeichnet. Alle übersetzten Wörter sind außerdem im Wörterverzeichnis im Anhang zusammengefasst.
Allein beim Schmökern im Roman können Sie sehr viel dazulernen. Vielleicht möchten Sie aber auch Ihr Grammatikwissen und Ihre Vokabelkenntnisse zusätzlich erweitern oder aber Ihr Textverständnis prüfen. Zu diesem Zweck finden Sie auf jeder Doppelseite knifflige und unterhaltsame Übungen. Die Vokabeln aus dem Text werden dort noch einmal verwendet und bleiben dadurch viel besser im Gedächtnis haften – so können Sie später leichter darauf zurückgreifen. Selbstverständlich sind auch die Lösungen zu allen Übungen im Anhang abgedruckt.

Und nun wünschen wir Ihnen viel Spaß beim Lesen!
Ihre Berlitz-Redaktion

1: The Club

I dressed a bit more speedily than normal on that snowy, windy, bitter night – I admit it. It was 23 December, 197 –, and I suspect that there were other members of the club who did the same. Taxis are notoriously hard to come by in New York on stormy nights, so I called for a radio-cab. I did this at five-thirty for an eight o'clock pick-up – my wife raised an eyebrow but said nothing. I was under the awning of the apartment building on East 58th Street, where Ellen and I had lived since 1946, by quarter to eight, and when the taxi was five minutes late, I found myself pacing up and down impatiently.

schnell

zu finden • Funktaxi • Abholen • Markise

The taxi arrived at 8.10 and I got in, too glad to be out of the wind to be as angry with the driver as he probably deserved. That wind, part of a cold front that had swept down from Canada the day before, meant business. It whistled and whined around the cab's window, occasionally drowning out the salsa on the driver's radio and rocking the big Checker* on its springs. Many of the stores were open but the sidewalks were nearly bare of last-minute shoppers. Those that were abroad looked uncomfortable or actually pained.

Kaltluftfront

meinte es ernst • übertönte • (amerikanisches Taxi)

draußen waren

It had been flurrying off and on all day, and now the snow began again, coming first in thin membranes, then twisting into cyclone shapes ahead of us in the street. Coming home that night, I would think of the combination of snow, a taxi, and New York City with considerably greater unease … but I did not of course know that then. At the corner of 3rd and Fortieth, a

es hatte Schneeschauer gegeben • Zyklonformen

Unbehagen

large tinsel Christmas bell went floating through the intersection like a spirit.

'Bad night,' the cabbie said. 'They'll have an extra two dozen in the morgue tomorrow. Wino Popsicles. Plus a few bag-lady Popsicles.'

'I suppose.'

The cabbie ruminated. 'Well, good riddance,' he said finally. 'Less welfare, right?'

'Your Christmas spirit,' I said, 'is stunning in its width and depth.'

The cabbie ruminated. 'You one of those bleeding-heart liberals?' he asked finally.

'I refuse to answer on the grounds that my answer might tend to incriminate me,' I said. The cabbie gave a why-do-I-always-get-the-wisenheimers snort … but he shut up.

He let me out at 2nd and Thirty-Fifth*, and I walked halfway down the block to the club, bent over against the whistling wind, holding my hat on my head with one gloved hand.

In almost no time at all the life-force seemed to have been driven deep into my body, a flickering blue flame about the size of the pilot-light in a gas oven. At seven-

aus Rauschgold

Taxifahrer • Leichenschauhaus • gefrorene Schnapsleichen • gefrorene Stadtstreicherinnen • sann darüber nach • Sozialhilfe • weichlich

belastend für mich ausfallen • Besserwisser

Lebenskraft

Zündflamme

info

Das New Yorker Straßenbild wurde über viele Jahrzehnte vom Checker Cab geprägt. Die gelben Limousinen mit der karierten (checkered) Bauchbinde wurden zwischen 1922 und 1982 von der Checker Motor Corporation in Kalamazoo, Michigan gebaut.

Amerikanische Städte sind in Rastern angelegt. In New York verlaufen die Straßen in Ost-West-Richtung mit ansteigender Nummer, ausgehend von der Houston Street in Manhattan. Allgemein gilt, dass avenues von Norden nach Süden verlaufen und streets von Osten nach Westen.

Groucho Marx ist ein amerikanischer Schauspieler und Entertainer.

ty-three, a man feels the cold quicker and deeper. That man should be home in front of a fireplace … or at least in front of an electric heater. At seventy-three, hot blood isn't even really a memory; it's more of an academic concept.

Kamin

The latest flurry was letting up, but snow as dry as sand still beat into my face. I was glad to see that the steps leading up to the door of 249 had been sanded – that was Stevens's work, of course – Stevens knew the base alchemy of old age well enough: not lead into gold but bones into glass. When I think about such things, I believe that God probably thinks a great deal like Groucho Marx*.

Schneeschauer • ließ nach • mit Sand gestreut worden waren • Alchemie

Then Stevens was there, holding the door open, and a moment later I was inside. Down the mahogany-panelled hallway, through double doors standing three-quarters of the way open on their recessed tracks, into the library *cum* reading-room *cum* bar. It was a dark room in which occasional pools of light gleamed – reading-lamps. A richer, more textured light glowed across the oak parquet floor, and I could hear the steady snap of birch logs in the huge fireplace. The heat radiated all the way across the room – surely there is no welcome for a man or a woman that can

mahagonigetäfelt • zurückgesetzt • Spuren • mit • Lichtinseln • texturiert • Parkettfußboden

strahlte … aus

Übung 1

Die folgenden Wörter bedeuten das Gegenteil von Wörtern auf dieser Doppelseite. Tragen Sie die gesuchten Wörter ein.

1. conservative ____________
2. question ____________
3. damp ____________
4. closed ____________
5. single ____________
6. tiny ____________
7. behind (Präposition) ____________

equal a fire on the hearth. A paper rustled – dry, slightly impatient. That would be Johanssen, with his *Wall Street Journal*. After ten years, it was possible to recognize his presence simply by the way he read his stocks. Amusing … and in a quiet way, amazing.

Kamin • raschelte • Börsenberichte

Stevens helped me off with my overcoat, murmuring that it was a dirty night; WCBS was now forecasting heavy snow before morning.

scheußlich • hätte … vorausgesagt

I agreed that it was indeed a dirty night and looked back into that big, high-ceilinged room again. A dirty night, a roaring fire … and a ghost story. Did I say that at seventy-three hot blood is a thing of the past? Perhaps so. But I felt something warm in my chest at the thought … something that hadn't been caused by the fire of Stevens's reliable, dignified welcome.

mit hoher Decke • lodernd • respektvoll

I think it was because it was McCarron's turn to tell the tale.

I had been coming to the brownstone which stands at 249 East 35th Street for ten years – coming at intervals that were almost – but not quite – regular. In my own mind I think of it as a 'gentleman's club', that amusing pre-Gloria Steinem* antiquity. But even now I am not sure that's what it really is, or how it came to be in the first place.

Haus aus rötlich-braunem Sandstein • Antiquität • gegründet wurde

On the night Emlyn McCarron told his story – the story of the Breathing Method – there were perhaps thirteen clubmembers in all, although only six of us had come out on that howling, bitter night. I can remember years when there might have been as few as eight full-time members, and others when there were at least twenty, and perhaps more.

Atemtechnik • heulend • Vollmitglieder

I suppose Stevens might know how it all came to be – one thing I *am* sure of is that Stevens has been there from the first, no matter how long that may be … and I believe Stevens to be older than he looks. Much, *much* older. He has a faint Brooklyn accent, but in

von Anfang an

spite of that he is as brutally correct and as cuttingly punctilious as a third-generation English butler. His reserve is part of his often maddening charm, and Stevens's small smile is a locked and latched door. I have never seen any club records – if he keeps them. I have never gotten a receipt of dues – there are no dues. I have never been called by the club secretary – there is no secretary, and at 249 East 55th, there are no phones. There is no box of white marbles and black balls. And the club – if it *is* a club – has never had a name.

gnadenlos förmlich • Zurückhaltung • verrückt machenden • verriegelt • Aufzeichnungen • Mitgliedsbeiträge • Murmeln

I first came to the club (as I must continue to call it) as the guest of George Waterhouse. Waterhouse headed the law firm for which I had worked since 1951. My progress upward in the firm – one of New York's three biggest – had been steady but extremely slow; I was a slogger, a mule for work, something of a centrepuncher … but I had no real flair or genius. I had seen men who had begun at the same time I had, promoted in giant steps while I only continued to pace – and I saw it with no real surprise.

Waterhouse and I had exchanged pleasantries, attended the obligatory dinner put on by the firm each Octo-

leitete

stetig • Arbeitstier • Arbeitspferd • jemand, der die Vorarbeit leistet • Talent • langsam vorankam • Höflichkeiten ausgetauscht

Übung 2

Sind die folgenden Aussagen wahr oder falsch? Tragen Sie ein T für true oder ein F für false in die Kästchen ein.

1. Stevens helps the narrator out of his jacket.
2. It is forecast to snow during the night.
3. Stevens started working at the club when it first opened.
4. The club is called 'The Brownstone Gentleman's Club'.
5. George Waterhouse is the club secretary.
6. The narrator works for a law firm.
7. The narrator is surprised that he hasn't been promoted more quickly.

info

Gloria Steinem ist eine amerikanische Feministin.

ber, and had little more congress until the fall of 196 –, when he dropped by my office one day in early November.

hatten uns kaum gesehen • Herbst • bei … hereinschaute • ausgeglichen • leichtsinnig • matt • in liebenswürdigem Ton über allgemeine Dinge • sich … zuzuwenden • Schriftsatz

This in itself was unusual enough, and it had me thinking black thoughts (dismissal) that were counterbalanced by giddy ones (an unexpected promotion). It was a puzzling visit. Waterhouse leaned in the doorway, his Phi Beta Kappa* key gleaming mellowly on his vest, and talked in amiable generalities – none of what he said seemed to have any real substance or importance. I kept expecting him to finish the pleasantries and get down to cases: 'Now about this Casey brief,' or 'We've been asked to research the Mayor's appointment of Salkowitz to –' But it seemed there *were* no cases. He glanced at his watch, said he had enjoyed our talk and that he had to be going.

verwirrt • alte Dummköpfe • einen feinen Gaumen haben

I was still blinking, bewildered, when he turned back and said casually: 'There's a place where I go most Thursday nights – a sort of club. Old duffers, mostly, but some of them are good company. They keep a really excellent cellar, if you've a palate. Every now and then someone tells a good story, as well. Why not come down some night, David? As my guest.'

info

Phi Beta Kappa ist eine US-amerikanische akademische Gemeinschaft, die im Jahr 1776 gegründet wurde. Sie gilt als älteste und angesehenste Honor Society bzw. studentische Vereinigung in den Vereinigten Staaten. Nur an etwa zehn Prozent der höheren Bildungsstätten der USA gibt es solche Gemeinschaften. In der Regel werden nicht mehr als zehn Prozent der Studenten aufgenommen. Das Symbol der Phi Beta Kappa ist ein goldener Schlüssel, auf dem drei Sterne, eine Hand und die Initialen PBK in griechischer Schrift stehen.

I stammered some reply – even now I'm not sure what it was. I was bewildered by the offer. It had a spur-of-the-moment sound, but there was nothing spur-of-the-moment about his eyes, blue Anglo-Saxon ice under the bushy white whorls of his eyebrows. And if I don't remember exactly how I replied, it was because I felt suddenly sure that this offer – vague and puzzling as it was – had been exactly the specific I had kept expecting him to get down to.

Ellen's reaction that evening was one of amused exasperation. I had been with Waterhouse, Carden, Lawton, Frasier, and Effingham for something like twenty years, and it was clear enough that I could not expect to rise much above the mid-level position I now held; it was her idea that this was the firm's cost-efficient substitute for a gold watch.

'Old men telling war stories and playing poker,' she said. 'A night of that and you're supposed to be happy in the Research Library until they pension you off, I suppose … oh, I put two Becks' on ice for you." And she kissed me warmly. I suppose she had seen something on my face – God knows she's good at reading me after all the years we've spent together.

stotterte • spontan

angelsächsisch • buschig • Wirbeln • rätselhaft • Einzelheit

Verzweiflung

wesentlich über … aufzusteigen • mittlere • kostengünstig • Ersatz

pensionieren

Übung 3

Die folgende Zusammenfassung des Textes dieser Doppelseite enthält drei sachliche Fehler. Können Sie sie finden und korrigieren?

Waterhouse visits the narrator in his office one day in the spring. He leans in the doorway and talks to the narrator about nothing of importance. The narrator expects him to go on to start talking about the cases they are working on, but he doesn't. Instead, he invites the narrator to go with him to a club which he goes to on Friday nights. The narrator is very puzzled by the offer. His wife thinks it means that they are going to promote him.

wochenlang	Nothing happened over a course of weeks. When my mind turned to Waterhouse's odd offer – certainly odd coming from a man with whom I met less than a dozen
ich mich … privat traf • mich über … getäuscht hatte	times a year, and who I only saw socially at perhaps three parties a year, including the company party in October – I supposed that I had been mistaken about the expression in his eyes, that he really had made the offer casually, and had forgotten it. Or regretted it – ouch! And then he approached me one late afternoon, a man of nearly seventy who was still broad-shouldered
zog … an • Überzieher	and athletic looking. I was shrugging on my topcoat with my briefcase between my feet. He said: 'If you'd still like to have a drink at the club, why not come tonight?' 'Well … I …'
drückte mir … in die Hand	'Good.' He slapped a slip of paper into my hand. 'Here's the address.' He was waiting for me at the foot of the steps that evening, and Stevens held the door for us. The wine
machte keinerlei Anstalten • Snobismus • bereute	was as excellent as Waterhouse had promised. He made no attempt whatsoever to 'introduce me around' – I took that for snobbery but later recanted the idea – but two or three of them introduced themselves to me.

Übung 4 Setzen Sie das Verb in den folgenden Sätzen jeweils in die Zeitform, die in Klammern steht.

1. The narrator clasped McCarron's hand briefly. (Präsens)

____

2. The narrator feels a lot out of place. (Imperfekt)

____

3. Waterhouse hadn't deserted the narrator. (Perfekt)

____

4. Waterhouse brings the narrator a drink. (Plusquamperfekt)

____

One of those who did so was Emlyn McCarron, even then in his early seventies. He held out his hand and I clasped it briefly. His skin was dry, leathery, tough; almost turtlelike. He asked me if I played bridge. I said I did not.

'God damned good thing,' he said. 'That god damned game has done more in this century to kill intelligent after-dinner conversation than anything else I can think of.' And with that pronouncement he walked away into the murk of the library, where shelves of books went up apparently to infinity.

I looked around for Waterhouse, but he had disappeared. Feeling a little uncomfortable and a lot out of place, I wandered over to the fireplace. It was, as I believe I have already mentioned, a huge thing – it seemed particularly huge in New York, where apartment-dwellers such as myself have trouble imagining such a benevolence big enough to do anything more than pop corn or toast bread. The fireplace at 249 East 35th was big enough to broil an ox whole. There was no mantle; instead a brawny stone arch curved over it. This arch was broken in the centre by a keystone which jutted out slightly. It was just on the level of my eyes, and although the light was dim, I could read the legend engraved on that stone with no trouble: *IT IS THE TALE, NOT HE WHO TELLS IT.*

'Here you go, David,' Waterhouse said from my elbow, and I jumped. He hadn't deserted me after all; had only trudged off into some uncharted locale to bring back drinks. 'Bombay martini's yours, isn't it?'

'Yes. Thank you. Mr Waterhouse –'

'George,' he said. 'Here it's just George.'

'George, then,' I said, although it seemed slightly mad to be using his first name. 'What is all of –'

'Cheers,' he said.

We drank. The martini was perfect. I said so instead of finishing my question.

drückte sie kurz • ledern • schildkrötenartig • gottverdammt

Feststellung • dämmrige Tiefe • ins Unendliche aufzuragen schienen • fehl am Platz

Apartmentbewohner • Feuerstelle • im Ganzen zu braten • Ummantelung • kräftig • Bogen • unterbrochen • Mittelstein • hervorragte

bitte schön • fuhr zusammen • im Stich gelassen • losgetrottet • unbekannt • Ort

ist Barkeeper • lebenswichtig • Fertigkeit • schwächte … ab • Desorientierung • Unsicherheit • Kleiderschrank • die … Smoking trugen • Holzfällerhemden • Kleidung • besonders

Trinkspruch • Formalitäten

dunkel

'Stevens tends the bar. He makes fine drinks. He likes to say it's a small but vital skill.'
The martini took the edge off my feelings of disorientation and awkwardness (the edge, but the feelings themselves remained – I had spent nearly half an hour gazing into my closet and wondering what to wear; I had finally settled on dark brown slacks and a rough tweed jacket that almost matched them, hoping I would not be wandering into a group of men either turned out in tuxedos or wearing bluejeans and L.L. Bean's lumberjack shirts … it seemed that I hadn't gone too far wrong on the matter of dress, anyway). A new place and a new situation makes one crucially aware of every social act, no matter how small, and at that moment, drink in hand and the obligatory small toast made, I wanted very much to be sure that I hadn't overlooked any of the amenities.
'Is there a guest book I ought to sign?' I asked. 'Something like that?'
He looked mildly surprised. 'We don't have anything like that,' he said. 'At least, I don't *think* we do.' He glanced around the dim, quiet room. Johanssen rattled his *Wall Street Journal*. I saw Stevens pass in a

Übung 5 Acht englische Begriffe sind in diesem Buchstabendickicht versteckt. Sie sind waagerecht, senkrecht oder diagonal angeordnet, aber jeweils von links nach rechts oder von rechts nach links sowie von oben nach unten oder umgekehrt!

Die deutschen Entsprechungen der Wörter lauten:

Gefühle	Funke
Gästebuch	Ahnung
obligatorisch	Gelb (einer Ampel)
geisterhaft	Scheit

doorway at the far end of the room, ghostly in his white messjacket. George put his drink on an endtable and tossed a fresh log onto the fire. Sparks corkscrewed up the black throat of the chimney.

'What does that mean?' I asked, pointing to the inscription on the keystone. 'Any idea?'

Waterhouse read it carefully, as if for the first time. *IT IS THE TALE, NOT HE WHO TELLS IT.*

'I suppose I have an idea,' he said. 'You may, too, if you should come back. Yes, I should say you may have an idea or two. In time. Enjoy yourself, David.'

He walked away. And, although it may seem odd, having been left to sink or swim in such an unfamiliar situation, I *did* enjoy myself. For one thing, I have always loved books, and there was a trove of interesting ones to examine here. I walked slowly along the shelves, examining the spines as best I could in the faint light, pulling one out now and then, and pausing once to look out a narrow window at the 2nd Avenue intersection up the street. I stood there and watched through the frost-rimmed glass as the traffic light at the intersection cycled from red to green to amber and back to red again, and quite suddenly I felt the queerest – and

Messjackett • kleiner Tisch • schob • stoben … hinauf • Inschrift

Nach und nach. • da ich im Stich gelassen wurde • Fundgrube

Buchrücken

von Eisblumen bedecktes Glas • von … wechselte • seltsamste

F	I	X	A	P	K	Y	O	F	R
U	T	E	V	F	O	G	B	E	E
K	D	L	O	G	O	T	L	E	B
I	R	T	F	K	B	D	I	L	M
H	N	A	U	H	T	K	G	I	A
A	C	A	P	C	S	B	A	N	Q
U	E	Y	S	S	E	K	T	G	W
R	W	Q	T	Q	U	N	O	S	H
M	J	O	D	Q	G	K	R	K	X
Y	L	T	S	O	H	G	Y	R	J

yet very welcome – sense of peace come to me. It did not flood in; instead it seemed to almost steal in. *Oh yes,* I can hear you saying, *that makes great sense; watching a stop-and-go light gives* everyone *a sense of peace.*

Das gebe ich zu. All right; it made *no* sense. I grant you that. But the feeling was there, just the same. It made me think for the first time in years of the winter nights in the Wisconsin farmhouse where I grew up: lying in bed in a

zugig • bemerkte • treibend draughty upstairs room and marking the contrast between the whistle of the January wind outside, drifting snow as dry as sand along miles of snow-fence, and

Steppdecken the warmth my body created under the two quilts.

There were some law books, but they were pretty damn

Zerstückelung strange: *Twenty Cases of Dismemberment and Their Outcomes under British Law* is one title I remember. *Pet Cases* was another. I opened that one and sure

Wälzer enough, it was a scholarly legal tome dealing with the law's treatment (American law, this time) of cases

betrafen which bore in some important respect upon pets – everything from housecats that had inherited great

Ozelot sums of money to an ocelot that had broken its chain and seriously injured a postman.

Gesamtausgabe There was a set of Dickens*, a set of Defoe*, a nearly endless set of Trollope*; and there was also a set of novels – eleven of them – by a man named Edward Gray Seville. They were bound in handsome green leather, and the name of the firm gold-stamped on the spine was Stedham & Son. I had never heard of Seville

Copyright nor of his publishers. The copyright date of the first Seville – *These Were Our Brothers* – was 1911. The date of the last, *Breakers*, was 1935.

Two shelves down from the set of Seville novels was a

Folioband large folio volume which contained careful step by step plans for Erector Set* enthusiasts. Next to it was another folio volume which featured famous scenes from famous movies. Each of these pictures filled one whole page, and opposite each, filling the facing pages, were free-verse poems either about the scenes with which they were paired or inspired by them. Not a very remarkable concept, but the poets who were represented *were* remarkable – Robert Frost*, Marianne Moore*, William Carlos Williams*, Wallace Stevens*, Louis Zukofsky*, and Erica Jong*, to mention just a few. Halfway through the book I found a poem by Archibald MacLeish set next to that famous photograph of Marilyn Monroe standing on the subway grating and trying to hold her skirt down. The poem was titled 'The Toll*' and it began:

The shape of the skirt is
– we would say –
the shape of a bell
The legs are the clapper –

And some such more. Not a terrible poem, but certainly not MacLeish's best or anywhere near the top drawer. I felt I could hold such an opinion because I had read a good deal of Archibald MacLeish over the years. I could not, however, recall this poem about Marilyn Monroe (which it is; the poem announces it even when divorced from the picture – at the end MacLeish writes: *My legs*

aus freien Versen • inspiriert

Gitter

Läuten

Klöppel

Spitzenklasse • mir ein solches Urteil erlauben • mich an … erinnern • getrennt

info

Die bekanntesten Romane der englischen Schriftsteller Charles Dickens (1812–1870), Daniel Defoe (1659–1731) und Anthony Trollope (1815–1882) sind Oliver Twist, Robinson Crusoe und The Chronicles of Barsetshire.

Erector sets sind beliebte Metallbaukästen aus den USA, mit denen man mit Werkzeugen und Schrauben Modelle zusammenbauen kann.

Frost, Moore, Williams, Stevens, Zukofsky und Jong sind alle aus den USA und schreiben moderne Gedichte.

Toll ist zweideutig. Es bedeutet entweder „Läuten“ oder „Tribut“.

clap my name:/Marilyn, ma belle). I have looked for it since then and haven't been able to find it ... which means nothing, of course. Poems are not like novels or legal opinions; they are more like blown leaves and any omnibus volume titled The Complete So-and-So must certainly be a lie. Poems have a way of getting lost under sofas – it is one of their charms, and one of the reasons they endure. But –

im Wind tanzend • die Gesamtausgabe von Soundso • beständig sind

At some point Stevens came by with a second martini (by then I had settled into a chair of my own with a volume of Ezra Pound). It was as perfect as the first. As I sipped it I saw two of those present, George Gregson and Harry Stein (Harry was six years dead on the night Emlyn McCarron told us the story of the Breathing Method), leave the room by a peculiar door less than three feet high. It was an Alice Down the Rabbit-Hole door if ever there was one. They left it open, and shortly after their odd exit from the library I heard the muted click of billiard balls.

hatte ... es mir in ... bequem gemacht

seltsam • Tür für Alice im Kaninchenbau • gedämpft • Klicken

Stevens passed by and asked if I would like another martini. I declined with real regret. He nodded. 'Very good, sir.' His face never changed, and yet I had an obscure feeling that I had somehow pleased him.

obskur

Übung 6 Beantworten Sie die Fragen zum Text. Welche Lösung ist die richtige?

1. The narrator thinks the billiards room door is peculiar because
a) it is very small.
b) it has no handle.
c) it is very wide.

2. When the narrator refuses a third martini, Stevens seems
a) pleased he said no.
b) to be furious with him.
c) to be laughing at him.

Laughter startled me from my book sometime later. Someone had thrown a packet of chemical powder into the fire and turned the flames momentarily parti-coloured. I though of my boyhood again … but not in any wistful, sloppily romantic-nostalgic way. I feel a great need to emphasize that, God knows why. I thought of times when I had done just such a thing as a kid, but the memory was a strong one, pleasant, untinged with regret.

I saw that most of the others had drawn chairs up around the hearth in a semi-circle. Stevens had produced a heaping, smoking platter of marvellous hot sausages. Harry Stein returned through the down-the-rabbit-hole door, introducing himself hurriedly but pleasantly to me. Gregson remained in the billiard room, practising shots, by the sound.

After a moment's hesitation I joined the others. A story was told – not a pleasant one. It was Norman Stett who told it, and while it is not my purpose to recount it here, perhaps you'll understand what I mean about its quality if I tell you that it was about a man who drowned in a telephone booth. When Stett – who is also dead now – finished, someone said, 'You should have saved it for

parti-coloured: teilweise farbig
wistful: wehmütig • sloppily: rührselig
untinged with: frei von
drawn up: herangezogen • semi-circle: Halbkreis • heaping: gehäuft • platter: Platte
recount: erzählen
drowned: ertrank

3. What sort of effect does the chemical powder have on the fire?

a) It causes a small explosion.
b) It causes a bad smell.
c) It causes the flames to change colour.

4. Why doesn't Gregson join the others round the hearth?

a) He wants to go to the bar.
b) He wants to practise playing billiards.
c) He has left the club.

Christmas, Norman.' There was laughter, which I of course did not understand. At least, not then.

Waterhouse himself spoke up then, and such a Waterhouse I never would have dreamed of in a thousand years of dreaming. A graduate of Yale, a Phi Beta Kappa, silver-haired, three-piece-suited head of a law firm so large it was more enterprise than company – *this* Waterhouse told a story that had to do with a teacher who had gotten stuck in a privy. The privy stood behind the one-room schoolhouse in which she had taught, and the day she got her caboose jammed into one of the privy's two holes also happened to be the day the privy was scheduled to be taken away as Anniston County's contribution to the Life As It Was in New England exhibition being held at the Prudential Center in Boston.

The teacher hadn't made a sound during all the time it took to load the privy onto the back of a flatbed truck and to spike it down; she was struck dumb with embarrassment and horror, Waterhouse said. And then the privy door blew off into the passing lane of Route 128 in Somerville during rush hour –

But draw a curtain over that, and over any other sto-

Absolvent der Yale-Universität • im Dreiteiler • Unternehmen • Klosett • mit ihrem Hinterteil … stecken blieb • der Tag, an dem das Klosett … abtransportiert werden sollte

Tieflader • befestigen • war vor … wie gelähmt • Überholspur • lassen wir das

Übung 7 Vervollständigen Sie die folgenden Sätze mit den passenden Präpositionen (at, for, of, with (2x))

1. The narrator would never have dreamed ____ such a Waterhouse before.
2. Waterhouse's story has to do _____ a teacher who got stuck in a privy.
3. The exhibition is being held ____ the Prudential Center.
4. The teacher was struck dumb _____ embarrassment.
5. The narrator thanks Waterhouse _____ inviting him to the club and sharing the cab.

ries which might have followed it; they are not my stories tonight. At some point Stevens produced a bottle of brandy that was more than just good; it was damned near exquisite. It was passed around and Johanssen raised a toast – *the* toast, one might almost say: The tale, not he who tells it.

We drank to that.

Not long after, men began slipping away. It wasn't late; not yet midnight, anyway; but I've noticed that when your fifties give way to your sixties, late begins coming earlier and earlier. I saw Waterhouse slipping his arms into the overcoat Stevens was holding open for him, and decided that must be my cue. I thought it strange that Waterhouse would slip away without so much as a word to me (which certainly seemed to be what he was doing; if I had come back from shelving the Pound book forty seconds later, he would have been gone), but no stranger than most of the other things that had gone on that evening.

I stepped out just behind him, and Waterhouse glanced around, as if surprised to see me … and almost as if he had been startled out of a light doze. 'Share a taxi?' he asked, as though we had just met by chance on this deserted, windy street.

'Thank you,' I said. I meant thanks for a great deal more than his offer to share a cab, and I believe that was unmistakable in my tone, but he nodded as if that was all I had meant. A taxi with its for-hire light lit was cruising slowly down the street – fellows like George Waterhouse seem to luck onto cabs even on those miserably cold or snowy New York nights when you would swear there isn't a cab to be had on the entire island of Manhattan – and he flagged it.

Inside, safely warm, the taxi-meter charting our journey in measured clicks, I told him how much I had enjoyed his story. I couldn't remember laughing so hard or so spontaneously since I was eighteen, I told

tranken darauf • sich davonzumachen

Einsatzzeichen

ins Regal zu stellen

aufgeschreckt • kleines Nickerchen

fuhr langsam • zufällig zu finden • zu finden • winkte … heran • maß

him, which was not flattery but only the simple truth. 'Oh? How kind of you to say.' His voice was chillingly polite. I subsided, feeling a dull flush in my cheeks. One does not always need to hear a slam to know that the door has been closed.

Schmeichelei • schrecklich • gab auf • Erröten • Zuschlagen • am Bordstein anhielt • kleines bisschen • so kurzfristig • legen wenig Wert auf Förmlichkeiten •

When the taxi drew up to the kerb in front of my building, I thanked him again, and this time he showed a trifle more warmth. 'It was good of you to come on such short notice,' he said. 'Come again, if you like. Don't wait for an invitation; we don't stand much on ceremony at two-four-nine. Thursdays are best for stories, but the club is there every night.'

Werde ich also Mitglied? • ich ließ es mir nur durch den Kopf gehen • Formulierung

Am I then to assume membership?

The question was on my lips. I meant to ask it; it seemed *necessary* to ask it. I was only mulling it over, listening to it in my head (in my tiresome lawyer's way) to hear if I had got the phrasing right – perhaps that was a little too blunt – when Waterhouse told the cabbie to drive on. The next moment the taxi was rolling on towards Madison. I stood there on the sidewalk for a moment, the hem of my topcoat whipping around my shins, thinking: *He knew I was going to ask that question – he knew it, and he purposely had the driver*

Bürgersteig • Saum

Übung 8 Tragen Sie die gesuchten Begriffe in das Kreuzworträtsel ein.

1. The opposite of 'difficult'.
2. A person who works in the legal profession.
3. The American equivalent of the British word 'pavement'.
4. The part of the body between the head and the shoulders.
5. The part of the body on each side of the face.
6. The noun which is derived from the adjective 'clear'.
7. Another word for a company.
8. To laugh at somebody.
9. The opposite of 'to tell a lie' would be 'to tell the _____'.
10. The opposite of 'long'.

go on before I could. Then I told myself that was utterly absurd – paranoid, even. And it was. But it was also true. I could scoff all I liked; none of the scoffing changed that essential certainty.

I walked slowly to the door of my building and went inside.

Ellen was sixty per cent asleep when I sat down on the bed to take off my shoes. She rolled over and made a fuzzy interrogative sound deep in her throat. I told her to go back to sleep.

She made the muzzy sound again. This time it approximated English: 'Howwuzzit?'

For a moment I hesitated, my shirt half-unbuttoned. And I thought with one moment's utter clarity: *If I tell her, I will never see the other side of that door again.*

'It was all right,' I said. 'Old men telling war stories.'

'I told you so.'

'But it wasn't bad. I might go back again. It might do me some good with the firm.'

'"The firm",' she mocked lightly. 'What an old buzzard you are, my love.'

'It takes one to know one,' I said, but she had already fallen asleep again. I undressed, showered, towelled,

völlig

spotten

undeutlich • fragend • unklar • ähnelte • Wie war's? • halb aufgeknöpft

spottete • Geier • nur ein Dieb kennt einen Dieb • trocknete mich ab

1	M
2	Y
3	S
4	T
5	E
6	R
7	I
8	O
9	U
10	S

put on my pyjamas … and then, instead of going to bed as I should have done (it was edging past one by that time), I put on my robe and had another bottle of Beck's. I sat at the kitchen table, drinking it slowly, looking out the window and up the cold canyon of Madison Avenue, thinking. My head was a trifle buzzy from my evening's intake of alcohol – for me an unexpectedly large intake. But the feeling was not at all unpleasant, and I had no sense of an impending hangover.

es war kurz nach eins • Bademantel

es summte ein bisschen in meinem Kopf • Alkoholkonsum • drohend

The thought which had come to me when Ellen asked me about my evening was as ridiculous as the one I'd entertained about George Waterhouse as the cab drew away from me – what in God's name could be wrong with telling my wife about a perfectly harmless evening at my boss's stuffy men's club … and even if something *were* wrong with telling her, who would know that I had? No, it was every bit as ridiculous and paranoid as those earlier musings … and, my heart told me, every bit as true.

lächerlich • hatte • losfuhr

steif

Überlegungen

I met George Waterhouse the next day in the hallway between Accounts and the Reading Library. Met him … Passed him would be more accurate. He nodded my way and went on without speaking … as he had done for years.

Buchhaltung • mir zu

My stomach muscles ached all day long. That was the only thing that completely convinced me the evening had been real.

Three weeks passed. Four … five. No second invitation came from Waterhouse. Somehow I just hadn't been right; hadn't fitted. Or so I told myself. It was a depressing, disappointing thought. I supposed it would begin to fade and lose its sting, as all disappointments eventually do. But I thought of that evening at the oddest

bedrückend • verblassen • seinen Stachel verlieren

moments – the isolated pools of library lamplight, so still and tranquil and somehow civilized; Waterhouse's absurd and hilarious tale of the schoolteacher stuck in the privy; the rich smell of leather in the narrow stacks. Most of all I thought of standing by that narrow window and watching the frost crystals change from green to amber to red. I thought of that sense of peace I had felt.

ruhig • urkomisch • Bücherregale

Eiskristalle

During that same five-week period I went to the library and checked out four volumes of Archibald MacLeish's poetry (I had three others myself, and had already checked through them); one of these volumes purported to be The Complete Poems of. I reacquainted myself with some old favourites, including my favourite MacLeish poem, 'Epistle to Be Left in Earth.' But I found no poem called 'The Toll' in any of the volumes. On that same trip to the New York Public Library, I checked the card catalogue for works of fiction by a man named Edward Gray Seville.

durchsuchte • durchsucht • sollte angeblich … sein • schloss neue Freundschaft mit • Epistel • Besuch • Romane

A mystery novel by a woman named Ruth Seville was the closest I came.

Come again, if you like; don't wait for an invitation …

Übung 9

Finden Sie die Wörter im Text, die das Gleiche bedeuten wie die folgenden Begriffe.

unhurriedly ________________
consumption ________________
sensation ________________
laughable ________________
reflections ________________
precise ________________
story ________________
tranquillity ________________

I was waiting for an invitation anyway, of course; my mother taught me donkey's years ago not to automatically believe people who tell you glibly to 'drop by anytime' or that 'the door is always open'. I didn't feel I needed an engraved card delivered to my apartment door by a footman in livery bearing a gilt plate, I don't mean that, but I did want *something*, even if it was only a casual remark: 'Coming by some night, David? Hope we didn't bore you.' That kind of thing.

vor langer Zeit • leichtfertig • vorbeizukommen • Diener • livriert • vergoldet

But when even that didn't come, I began to think more seriously about going back anyway – after all, sometimes people really *did* want you to drop in anytime; I supposed that, at some places, the door always *was* open; and that mothers weren't always right.

vorbeizukommen

... don't wait for an invitation ...

Anyway, that's how it happened that, on 10 December of that year, I found myself putting on my rough tweed coat and dark brown pants again and looking for my darkish red tie. I was rather more aware of my heartbeat than usual that night, I remember.

'George Waterhouse finally broke down and asked you back?' Ellen asked. 'Back into the sty with the rest of the male chauvinist oinkers?'

Hose • dunkel • hat sein Schweigen gebrochen • Schweinestall • Grunzer

Übung 10 In allen gesuchten Wörtern steckt der Buchstabe „e". Finden Sie die englischen Begriffe mithilfe der Erklärungen und Hinweise.

1. The twelfth month of the year.
2. To be sure that something is true.
3. A rough woollen cloth used to make jackets.
4. The action of the large organ in your chest which pumps blood round the body.
5. An occasion on which two or more people come together.
6. Happy anticipation.

'That's right,' I said, thinking it must be the first time in at least a dozen years that I had told her a lie … and then I remembered that, after the first meeting, I had answered her questions about what it had been like with a lie. Old men telling war stories, I had said.
'Well, maybe there really *will* be a promotion in it,' she said … though without much hope. To her credit, she said it without much bitterness, either.
'Stranger things have happened,' I said, and kissed her goodbye. 'Oink-oink,' she said as I went out the door.
The taxi ride that night seemed very long. It was cold, still, and starry. The cab was a Checker and I felt somehow very small in it, like a child seeing the city for the first time. It was excitement I was feeling as the cab pulled up in front of the brownstone – something as simple and yet complete as that. But such simple excitement seems to be one of life's qualities that slips away almost unnoticed, and its rediscovery as one grows older is always something of a surprise, like finding a black hair or two in one's comb years after one had last found such a thing.
I paid the driver, got out, and walked towards the four steps leading to the door. As I mounted them, my

sie belogen hatte
springt dabei … heraus • es machte ihr große Ehre • grunz, grunz
sternenklar
hielt • vollkommen • verloren gehen • unbemerkt
hinaufstieg

1. _ e _ e _ _ e _

2. _ e _ _ e _ e

3. _ _ e e _

4. _ e _ _ _ _ e _ _

5. _ e e _ _ _ _

6. e _ _ _ _ e _ e _ _

zu … gerann • Angst

excitement curdled into plain apprehension (a feeling the old are much more familiar with). What exactly was I doing here?

unüberwindlich • Festungsturm • Überwachungskamera • unauffällig angebracht • Dachgesims • die man besser nicht lüftete

The door was of thick panelled oak, and to my eye it looked as stout as the door of a castle keep. There was no doorbell that I could see, no knocker, no closed circuit TV camera mounted unobtrusively in the shadow of a deep eave, and, of course, no Waterhouse waiting to take me in. I stopped at the foot of the steps and looked around. Thirty-Fifth Street suddenly seemed darker, colder, more threatening. The brownstones all looked somehow secret, as if hiding mysteries best not investigated. Their windows looked like eyes.

der … plant • Es lief mir kalt den Rücken hinunter. • Woge • besonders • gespenstisch • mit etwas herausgeplatzt

Somewhere, behind one of those windows, there may be a man or woman contemplating murder, I thought. *A shudder worked up my spine. Contemplating it … or doing it.*

Then, suddenly, the door was open and Stevens was there.

I felt an intense surge of relief. I am not an overly imaginative man, I think – at least not under ordinary circumstances – but this last thought had had all the eerie clarity of prophecy. I might have babbled aloud if

Übung 11 Ergänzen Sie die fehlenden Wörter aus den jeweiligen Wortfamilien, die auch im Text auf dieser Doppelseite zu finden sind.

Noun	Verb	Adjective
threat	to threaten	
opening	to open	
imagination	to imagine	
dullness		dull
	to embarrass	embarrassing
	to humiliate	humiliating

I hadn't glanced at Stevens's eyes first. His eyes did not know me. His eyes did not know me at all.

Then there was another instance of that eerie, prophetic clarity; I saw the rest of my evening in perfect detail. Three hours in a quiet bar. Three martinis (perhaps four) to dull the embarrassment of having been fool enough to go where I wasn't wanted. The humiliation my mother's advice had been intended to avoid – that which comes with knowing one has overstepped. I saw myself going home a little tipsy, but not in a good way. I saw myself merely sitting through the cab ride rather than experiencing it through that childlike lens of excitement and anticipation. I heard myself saying to Ellen, *It wears thin after a while … Waterhouse told the same story about winning a consignment of T-bone steaks for the 3rd Battalion in a poker game … and they play Hearts for a dollar a point, can you believe it? … go back? … I suppose I might, but I doubt it.* And that would be the end of it. Except, I suppose, for my own humiliation.

I saw all of this in the nothing of Stevens's eyes. Then the eyes warmed. He smiled slightly and said: 'Mr Adley! Come in. I'll take your coat.'

I mounted the steps and Stevens closed the door firmly behind me. How different a door can feel when you are on the warm side of it! He took my coat and was gone with it. I stood in the hall for a moment, looking at my own reflection in the pier glass, a man of sixty-three whose face was rapidly becoming too gaunt to look middle-aged. And yet the reflection pleased me.

I slipped into the library.

Johanssen was there, reading his *Wall Street Journal.* In another island of light, Emlyn McCarron sat over a chessboard opposite Peter Andrews. McCarron was and is a cadaverous man, possessed of a narrow, bladelike nose; Andrews was huge, slope-shouldered, and choleric. A vast ginger-coloured beard sprayed over his

Anfall

lindern • weil ich dumm genug gewesen war • Demütigung • zu weit gegangen ist • beschwipst • Linse • es wird langsam langweilig • Wagenladung

Spiegelbild • (Art großer Spiegel) • hager

ausgezehrt • scharf • mit abfallenden Schultern • wucherte

Brett mit Einlegearbeit • Elfenbein • Ebenholz

vest. Face to face over the inlaid board with its carved pieces of ivory and ebony, they looked like Indian totems: eagle and bear.

Waterhouse was there, frowning over that day's *Times*. He glanced up, nodded at me without surprise, and disappeared into the paper again.

unaufgefordert • verlockend

Stevens brought me a Bombay martini, unasked.

I took it into the stacks and found that puzzling, enticing set of green volumes again. I began reading the works of Edward Gray Seville that night. I started at the beginning, with *These Were Our Brothers*. Since then I have read them all, and believe them to be eleven of the finest novels of our century.

halte sie für

Near the end of the evening there was a story – just one – and Stevens brought brandy around. When the tale was told, people began to rise, preparing to leave. Stevens spoke from the double doorway which communicated with the hallway. His voice was low and pleasant, but carrying:

aufzustehen • Doppeltür • zu … führte • leise • deutlich

'Who will bring us a tale for Christmas, then?'

People stopped what they were doing and glanced around. There was some low, goodnatured talk and a burst of laughter.

freundlich

Übung 12 Welche Satzteile passen zusammen? Tragen Sie die entsprechenden Buchstaben in die Kästchen ein.

1. I was a little disappointed
2. Since then I have read them all
3. There was some low, goodnatured talk
4. Cold draughts swirled up the hallway
5. I took it into the stacks
6. Near the end of the evening there was a story – just one –

Stevens, smiling but serious, clapped his hands together twice, like a grammar school teacher calling an unruly class to order. 'Come, gentlemen – who'll bring the tale?'

Gymnasiallehrer • undiszipliniert

Peter Andrews, he of the sloped shoulders and gingery beard, cleared his throat. 'I have something I've been thinking about. I don't know if it's quite right; that is, if it's –'

rötlich • räusperte sich

'That will be fine,' Stevens interrupted, and there was more laughter. Andrews had his back slapped good naturedly. Cold draughts swirled up the hallway as men slipped out.

freundschaftlich • Luftzüge • wirbelten … entlang

Then Stevens was there, as if by benign magic, holding my coat, for me. 'Good evening, Mr Adley. Always a pleasure.'

gutartig

'Do you really meet on Christmas night?' I asked, buttoning my coat. I was a little disappointed that I was going to miss Andrews's story, but we had made firm plans to drive to Schenectady and keep the holiday with Ellen's sister. Stevens managed to look both shocked and amused at the same time. 'In no case,' he said. 'Christmas is a night a man should spend with his family. That night, if no other. Don't you agree, sir?'

als ich … zuknöpfte • fest • zu verbringen • aber nein

a) as men slipped out.

b) that I was going to miss Andrews' story.

c) and Stevens brought brandy around.

d) and found that puzzling, enticing set of green volumes again.

e) and believe them to be eleven of the finest novels of our century.

f) and a burst of laughter.

an dem uns eine hohe Teilnehmerzahl sicher ist • Zufall • Vermeidung • erzählt • Übernatürliche • nämlich, dass • lagen • Warnung • Verstehen Sie mich? • eher • Knorren • flutete • noch unbekannt • dumpf • Aufschlag • sicher • trat über die Schwelle • grässlich

'I certainly do.'

'We always meet on the Thursday before Christmas. In fact, that is the one night of the year when we're assured a large turnout.'

He hadn't used the word *members*, I noticed – just happenstance or neat avoidance?

'Many tales have been spun out in the main room, Mr Adley, tales of every sort, from the comic to the tragic to the ironic to the sentimental. But on the Thursday before Christmas, it's always a tale of the uncanny. It's always been that way, at least as far back as I can remember.'

That at least explained the comment I had heard on my first visit, the one to the effect that Norman Stett should have saved his story for Christmas. Other questions hovered on my lips, but I saw a reflected caution in Stevens's eyes. Do you catch my drift? It was not a warning that he would not answer my questions; it was, rather, a warning that I should not even ask them.

'Was there something else, Mr Adley?'

We were alone in the hall now. All the others had left. And suddenly the hallway seemed darker, Stevens's long face paler, his lips redder.

A knot exploded in the fireplace and a red glow washed momentarily across the polished parquet floor. I thought I heard, from somewhere in those as-yet-unexplored rooms beyond, a kind of slithery bump. I did not like the sound.

'No,' I said in a voice that was not quite steady. 'I think not.'

'Goodnight, then,' Stevens said, and I crossed the threshold. I heard the heavy door close behind me. I heard the lock turn.

And then I was walking towards the lights of 2nd Avenue, not looking back over my shoulder, somehow afraid to look back, as if I might see some frightful fiend matching me stride for stride, or glimpse some secret better kept than known. I reached the corner, saw an empty cab, and flagged it.

Teufel • der mit mir Schritt hielt • flüchtig sehen • bewahrt

'More war stories?' Ellen asked me that night. She was in bed with Philip Marlowe*, the only lover she has ever taken.

hatte

'There was a war story or two,' I said, hanging up my overcoat. 'Mostly I sat and read a book.'

'When you weren't oinking.'

nicht beim Grunzen warst •

'Yes, that's right. When I wasn't oinking.'

'Listen to this: "*The first time I ever laid eyes on Terry Lennox he was drunk in a Rolls-Royce Silver Wraith outside the terrace of the Dancers,*"' Ellen read. '"*He had a young-looking face but his hair was bone white. You could tell by his eyes that he was plastered to the hairline, but otherwise he looked like any other nice young guy in a dinner jacket who had been spending too much money in a place that exists for that purpose and for no other.*" Nice, huh? It's –'

zu Gesicht bekam

schlohweiß • blau war wie ein Veilchen • Smokingjacke

nicht wahr?

'*The Long Goodbye**,' I said, taking off my shoes. 'You read me that same passage once every three years. It's part of your life-cycle.'

Lebenszyklus

info

Philip Marlowe ist eine Figur in den Romanen des amerikanischen Schriftstellers Raymond Chandler. Marlowe ist der Prototyp des Privatdetektivs, der in einer unmoralischen Welt seine moralische Integrität zu bewahren versucht. Oft wendet er unkonventionelle Methoden an, um seine Fälle zu lösen, und obwohl er ein knallharter Typ ist, hat er auch seine sentimentale Seite. The Long Goodbye ist einer der bekanntesten Romane mit Philip Marlowe. Er wurde 1953 veröffentlicht und 1973 verfilmt. Von den anderen Verfilmungen von Chandlers Romanen ist The Big Sleep (1946) die bekannteste. Die Hauptrolle von Philip Marlowe wird im Film von Humphrey Bogart gespielt.

rümpfte die Nase

She wrinkled her nose at me. 'Oink-oink.'

'Thank you,' I said.

Bettdecke • prüfend • beitreten

She went back to her book. I went out into the kitchen to get a bottle of Beck's. When I came back, she had laid *The Long Goodbye* open on the counterpane and was looking at me closely. 'David, are you going to join this club?'

'I suppose I might … if I'm asked.' I felt uncomfortable. I had perhaps told her another lie. If there was such a thing as membership at 249 East 35th, I already was a member.

Sozialhilfeausschuss • Frauenrechtskommission • Theaterverein • brandneu • gebunden

'I'm glad,' she said. 'You've needed something for a long time now. I don't think you even know it, but you have. I've got the Relief Committee and the Commission on Women's Rights and the Theatre Society. But you've needed something. Some people to grow old with, I think.'

I went to the bed and sat beside her and picked up *The Long Goodbye*. It was a bright, new-minted paperback. I could remember buying the original hardback edition as a birthday present for Ellen. In 1953. 'Are we old?' I asked her.

Übung 13 Die folgenden Sätze enthalten jeweils einen grammatischen Fehler. Suchen und korrigieren Sie ihn.

1. The narrator feels as if he is already member of the club.
2. Ellen thinks he's needed something to occupy him since a long time.
3. The narrator goes to sits beside Ellen on the bed.
4. He can remember buy the original hardback edition of the book.
5. There are more peoples than usual at the club on the Thursday before Christmas.
6. The narrator and the other men talk from this and that.

'I suspect we are,' she said, and smiled brilliantly at me.
I put the book down and touched her breast. 'Too old for this?'
She turned the covers back with ladylike decorum … and then, giggling, kicked them onto the floor with her feet. 'Beat me, daddy,' Ellen said, 'eight to the bar.'
'Oink, oink,' I said, and then we were both laughing.

The Thursday before Christmas came. That evening was much the same as the others, with two notable exceptions. There were more people there, perhaps as many as eighteen. And there was a sharp, indefinable sense of excitement in the air. Johanssen took only a cursory glance at his *Journal* and then joined McCarron, Hugh Beagleman, and myself. We sat near the windows, talking of this and that, and finally fell into a passionate – and often hilarious – discussion of pre-war automobiles.
There was, now that I think of it, a third difference as well – Stevens had concocted a delicious eggnog punch. It was smooth, but it was also hot with rum and spices. It was served from an incredible Waterford

strahlend

schlug … zurück • Bettdecke • damenhaft • Grazie • hau mich • aber im Takt •

bemerkenswert

undefinierbar

flüchtig • gesellte sich zu • fingen an … zu diskutieren

gezaubert • Eierpunsch • mild

Übung 14

Bringen Sie die Buchstaben der Wörter in Klammern in die richtige Reihenfolge und vervollständigen Sie die folgenden Sätze.

1. The narrator goes out into the ___________ (nikthec) to get some beer.
2. Ellen's book is a brand new ___________ (kppraabce) edition.
3. The narrator bought the original hardback edition for Ellen as a ___________ ___________ (ybaidhtr nseeptr).
4. The narrator finds Stevens's eggnog punch ___________ (ocdlusiie).

bowl that looked like an ice-sculpture, and the animated hum of the conversation grew ever higher as the level of the punch grew lower.

I looked over in the corner by the tiny door leading to the billiard room and was astounded to see Waterhouse and Norman Stett flipping baseball cards into what looked like a genuine beaver tophat. They were laughing uproariously.

Groups formed and re-formed. The hour grew late … and then, at the time when people usually began slipping out through the front door, I saw Peter Andrews seated in front of the fire with an unmarked packet, about the size of a seed envelope, in one hand. He tossed it into the flames without opening it, and a moment later the fire began to dance with every colour of the spectrum – and some, I would have sworn, from outside it – before turning yellow again. Chairs were dragged around. Over Andrews's shoulder I could see the keystone with its etched homily: *IT IS THE TALE, NOT HE WHO TELLS IT.*

Stevens passed unobtrusively among us, taking punch glasses and replacing them with snifters of brandy. There were murmurs of 'Merry Christmas' and 'Top of

angeregt • Summen • Pegel
erstaunt • werfen • Zylinderhut aus Biberpelz • lärmend
unbedruckt • Samentüte
geschworen
Spruch • unaufdringlich • Schwenker • schöne Feiertage

info

Ebenezer Scrooge ist die Hauptfigur in Charles Dickens Roman A Christmas Carol („Eine Weihnachtsgeschichte"). Scrooge wandelt sich im Roman vom geizigen Geschäftemacher zu einem großzügigen und warmherzigen alten Mann, nachdem er am Heiligen Abend vom Geist seines ehemaligen Geschäftspartners Jacob Marley und von den Geistern der vergangenen, gegenwärtigen und künftigen Weihnacht besucht wird. Sie weisen ihn darauf hin, dass seine Lebensweise ihm die ewige Verdammnis einbringt, wenn er sie nicht ändert. Die Szene, die auf dieser Doppelseite erwähnt wird, spielt am frühen Weihnachtstag nach Scrooges Verwandlung. Der Roman wurde so bekannt, dass der Name „Scrooge" heutzutage ein allgemeiner Begriff für „Geizhals" ist.

the season, Stevens,' and for the first time I saw money change hands – a ten dollar bill was unobtrusively tendered here, a bill that looked like a fifty there, one which I clearly saw was a hundred from another chair. 'Thank you, Mr McCarron … Mr Johanssen … Mr Beagleman …' A quiet, well-bred murmur.	den Besitzer wechseln • Schein • gegeben wohlerzogen
I have lived in New York long enough to know that the Christmas season is a carnival of tips; something for the butcher, the baker, the candlestick-maker – not to mention the doorman, the super, and the cleaning lady who comes in Tuesdays and Fridays. I've never met anyone of my own class who regarded this as anything but a necessary nuisance … but I felt none of that grudging spirit on that night. The money was given willingly, even eagerly … and suddenly, for no reason (it was the way thoughts often seemed to come when one was at 249), I thought of the boy calling up to Scrooge* on the still, cold air of a London Christmas morning: 'Wot? The goose that's as big as me?' And Scrooge, nearly crazed with joy, giggling '*A good* boy! An *excellent* boy!'	Trinkgelder • Kerzenmacher • Portier • Hausmeister • gesellschaftliche Stellung • Übel • Widerwillen • gern • mit Eifer Was? • verrückt
I found my own wallet. In the back of this, behind the pictures of Ellen I keep, there has always been a fifty dollar bill which I keep for emergencies. When Stevens gave me my brandy, I slipped it into his hand with never a qualm … although I was not a rich man.	Notfälle • ohne das geringste Bedauern
'Happy Christmas, Stevens,' I said.	
'Thank you, sir. And the same to you.'	
He finished passing out the brandies and collecting his honorariums and retired. I glanced around once, at the midpoint of Peter Andrews's story, and saw him standing by the double doors, a dim manlike shadow, still and silent.	Honorare • mitten in
'I'm a lawyer now, as most of you know,' Andrews said after sipping at his glass, clearing his throat, and then sipping again. 'I've had offices on Park Avenue for the last twenty-two years. But before that, I was a legal	an … genippt hatte

musste ich Überstunden machen • Fallzitate in den Index aufzunehmen • blutgetränkt • fielen ihm fast aus dem Kopf

assistant in a firm of lawyers which did business in Washington, DC. One night in July I was required to stay late in order to finish indexing case citations in a brief which hasn't anything at all to do with this story. But then a man came in – a man who was at that time one of the most widely known Senators on the Hill*, a man who later almost became President. His shirt was matted with blood and his eyes were bulging from their sockets.

auf dem privaten Sektor

"I've got to talk to Joe," he said. Joe, you understand, was Joseph Woods, the head of my firm, one of the most influential private-sector lawyers in Washington, and this Senator's close personal friend.

Messerstecherei • (Fernsehsendung) • blutverschmiert • zuckte • fingerte am … herum • an … weiterzugeben

"He went home hours ago," I said. I was terribly frightened, I can tell you – he looked like a man who had just walked away from a dreadful car accident, or perhaps from a knife-fight. And somehow seeing his face which I had seen in newspaper photos and on *Meet the Press* – seeing it streaked with gore, one cheek twitching spasmodically below one wild eye … all of that made my fright worse. "I can call him if you –" I was already fumbling with the phone, mad with eagerness to turn this unexpected responsibility over to someone else.

info

Das Kapitol ist der Sitz des US-Kongresses in Washington DC. Es wurde 1791 auf dem Jenkins Hill gebaut, der später in Capitol Hill umbenannt wurde. Diese Bezeichnung leitet sich vom Kapitolinischen Hügel, dem wichtigsten der sieben Hügel Roms, ab. Im Kapitol finden Sitzungen des Senats (Senate) und des Repräsentantenhauses (House of Representatives) statt. Da sich Capitol Hill nicht nur auf den Sitz des Kongresses, sondern auch auf den Kongress selbst beziehen kann, bedeutet der Zusatz „on the Hill" im Text auf dieser Doppelseite „im Kongress".

Looking behind him, I could see the caked and bloody footprints he had left on the carpet. — verkrustet

'"I've got to talk to Joe right now," he reiterated as if he hadn't heard me.' "There's something in the trunk of my car ... something I found out at the Virginia place. I've shot it and stabbed it and I can't kill it. It's not human, and I can't kill it." — wiederholte • Kofferraum • eingestochen

'He began to giggle ... and then to laugh ... and finally to scream. And he was still screaming when I finally got Mr Woods on the phone and told him to come, for God's sake, to come as fast as he could ...' — am Apparat hatte

It is not my purpose to tell Peter Andrews's story, either. As a matter of fact, I am not sure I would dare to tell it. Suffice it to say that it was a tale so gruesome that I dreamed of it for weeks afterwards, and Ellen once looked at me over the breakfast table and asked me why I had suddenly cried out 'His head! His head is still speaking in the earth!' in the middle of the night. — ehrlich gesagt • es reicht wohl, wenn ich sage • grausig • geschrien

'I suppose it was a dream,' I said. 'One of those you can't remember afterwards.'

But my eyes dropped immediately to my coffee cup, and I think that Ellen knew the lie that time. — Blick sank

Übung 15

Welche Wörter gehören zusammen? Verbinden Sie sie mit einer Linie.

private	table
car	friend
personal	cup
knife	sector
newspaper	accident
breakfast	fight
coffee	photos

One day in August of the following year, I was buzzed as I worked in the Readers' Library. It was George Waterhouse. He asked me if I could step up to his office. When I got there I saw that Robert Carden was also there, and Henry Effingham. For one moment I was positive I was about to be accused of some really dreadful act of stupidity or malfeasance.

Then Carden stepped around to me and said: 'George believes the time has come to make you a junior partner, David. The rest of us agree.'

'It's going to be a little bit like being the world's oldest JayCee,' Effingham said with a grin, 'but it's the channel you have to go through, David. With any luck, we can make you a full partner by Christmas.'

There were no bad dreams that night. Ellen and I went out to dinner, drank too much, went on to a jazz place where we hadn't been in nearly six years, and listened to that amazing blue-eyed black man, Dexter Gordon, blow his horn until almost two in the morning. We woke up the next morning with fluttery stomachs and achey heads, both of us still unable to completely believe what had happened. One of them was that my salary had just climbed by eight thousand dollars a year long after our expectations of such a staggering income jump had fallen by the wayside.

The firm sent me to Copenhagen for six weeks that fall, and I returned to discover that John Hanrahan, one of the regular attendees at 249, had died of cancer. A collection was taken up for his wife, who had been left in unpleasant circumstances. I was pressed into service to total the amount – which was given entirely in cash – and convert it to a cashier's check. It came to almost ten thousand dollars. I turned the check over to Stevens and I suppose he mailed it.

It just so happened that Arlene Hanrahan was a member of Ellen's Theatre Society, and Ellen told me some time later that Arlene had received an anonymous

rief man mich
zu … kommen
sicher • vorgeworfen • Dummheit • Vergehen • die Zeit sei reif
Junior • Dienstweg
gingen nachher zu
verstimmt • Kopfschmerzen • sich gerade um … erhöht hatte • umwerfend • sprunghafter Einkommensanstieg • begraben wurden • Besucher • eine Sammlung wurde durchgeführt • wurde gebeten • zusammenzuzählen • umzutauschen • Bankscheck • anonym

check for ten thousand four hundred dollars. Written on the check stub was the brief and unilluminating message 'Friends of your late husband John.'

'Isn't that the most amazing thing you ever heard in your *life*?' Ellen asked me.

'No,' I said, 'but it's right up there in the top ten. Are there any more strawberries, Ellen?'

Abschnitt • kurz • wenig informativ

es gehört zu den zehn merkwürdigsten •

The years went by. I discovered a warren of rooms upstairs at 249 – a writing room, a bedroom where guests sometimes stayed overnight (although after that slithery bump I had heard – or imagined I had heard – I believe I personally would rather have registered at a good hotel), a small but well-equipped gymnasium, and a sauna bath. There was also a long, narrow room which ran the length of the building and contained two bowling alleys.

In those same years I re-read the novels of Edward Gray Seville, and discovered an absolutely stunning poet – the equal of Ezra Pound and Wallace Stevens, perhaps – named Norbert Rosen. According to the back flap on one of the three volumes of his work in the stacks, he had been born in 1924 and killed at Anzio.

Labyrinth

mich in ... angemeldet • gut ausgerüstet • Fitnessraum • sich über die ganze Länge ... erstreckte • Kegelbahnen • atemberaubend • Rücken

Übung 16

Welches der angegebenen Wörter passt in die Lücke?

1. Becoming a junior partner means the narrator's salary will rise _____ eight thousand dollars a year.
with by on

2. The club members take up a __________ for Hanrahan's wife.
bouquet card collection

3. Arlene Hanrahan is a member _____ Ellen's Theatre Society.
of in from

All three volumes of his work had been published by Stedham & Son, New York and Boston.

I remember going back to the New York Public Library on a bright spring afternoon during one of those years (of which year I am no longer sure) and requesting twenty years' worth of Literary Market Place. The LMP is an annual publication the size of a large city's Yellow Pages, and the reference room librarian was quite put out with me, I'm afraid. But I persisted, and went through each volume carefully. And although LMP is supposed to list every publisher, great and small, in the United States (in addition to agents, editors, and book club staffs), I found no listing for Stedham & Son. A year later – or perhaps it was two years later – I fell into conversation with an antiquarian book dealer and asked him about the imprint. He said he had never heard of it.

I thought of asking Stevens – saw that warning light in his eyes – and dropped the question unasked.

sonnig • verlangte • erscheint jährlich • Raum für Nachschlagewerke • Bibliothekar • böse auf • ließ nicht locker • Personal • war … nicht aufgeführt • kam ich … ins Gespräch • Antiquar • Impressum

And, over those years, there were stories.

Tales, to use Stevens's word. Funny tales, tales of love found and love lost, tales of unease. Yes, and even a few

unheimliche Geschichten

Übung 17 Kreuzen Sie den Begriff an, der nicht zu den anderen passt.

1. Which of the following words has <u>nothing</u> to do with books?

☐ graduate	☐ librarian
☐ imprint	☐ publication

2. Which of the following words does <u>not</u> mean 'wahnsinnig'?

☐ mad	☐ goodnatured
☐ crazy	☐ insane

war stories, although none of the sort Ellen had likely been thinking of when she made the suggestion.
I remember Gerard Tozeman's story the most clearly – the tale of an American base of operations which took a direct hit from German artillery four months before the end of World War I, killing everyone present except for Tozeman himself.
Lathrop Carruthers, the American general who everyone had by then decided must be utterly insane (he had been responsible for better than eighteen *thousand* casualties by then – lives and limbs spent as casually as you or I might spend a quarter in a jukebox), was standing at a map of the front lines when the shell struck. He had been explaining yet another mad flanking operation at that moment – an operation which would have succeeded only on the level of all the others Carruthers had hatched: it would be wonderfully successful at making new widows.
And when the dust cleared, Gerard Tozeman, dazed and deaf, bleeding from his nose, his ears, and the corners of both eyes, his testicles already swelling from the force of the concussion, had come upon Carruthers's body while looking for a way out of the abbatoir

Operationsbasis • Volltreffer

wahnsinnig • mehr als • Tote und Verwundete • Vierteldollar • Granate • Flankenoperation • genauso wie • ausgeheckt • sich verzogen hatte • benommen • Hoden • Gewalt • Aufprall • Schlachthof

3. Which of the following things are <u>not</u> listed in the LMP?

editors	lawyers
agents	publishers

4. Which of the following words has <u>nothing</u> to do with warfare?

general	artillery
sidewalk	shell

5. Which of the following words is <u>not</u> a part of the human body?

awning	limb
ear	nose

that had been the staff HQ only minutes before. He looked at the general's body … and then began to scream and laugh. The sounds went unheard by his own shellshocked ears, but they served to notify the medicos that someone was still alive in that strew of matchwood.

Carruthers had not been mutilated by the blast … at least, Tozeman said, it hadn't been what the soldiers of that long-ago war had come to think of as mutilation – men whose arms had been blown off, men with no feet, no eyes; men whose lungs had been shrivelled by gas.

No, he said, it was nothing like that. The man's mother would have known him at once. But the map …

… the map before which Carruthers had been standing with his butcher's pointer when the shell struck …

It had somehow *been driven into his face*. Tozeman had found himself staring into a hideous, tattooed deathmask. Here was the stony shore of Britanny on the bony ridge of Lathrop Carruthers's brow. Here was the Rhine flowing like a blue scar down his left cheek. Here were some of the finest wine-growing provinces

Stab • von der Detonation betäubt • Sanitäter • verstreutes Kleinholz • verstümmelt • abgerissen • geschrumpft • Zeigestock • getrieben • grässlich • tätowiert • felsig • Küste • Carruthers Stirn • Weinanbaugebiete

Übung 18 In jeder Zeile steht ein Wort, das nicht zu den anderen passt. Streichen Sie es durch.

1. foot – brow – chin – cheek
2. poem – story – song – tale
3. taxi – bus – train – bike
4. change – purse – coin – bill
5. huge – enormous – leathery – gigantic
6. Christmas – New Year's Eve – Advent – Thanksgiving

in the world bumped and ridged over his chin. Here was the Saar drawn around his throat like a hangman's noose … and printed across one bulging eyeball was the word VERSAILLES.

That was our Christmas story in the year 197 –.

I remember many others, but they do not belong here. Properly speaking, Tozeman's doesn't, either … but it was the first 'Christmas tale' I heard at 249, and I could not resist telling it. And then, on the Thursday after Thanksgiving of this year, when Stevens clapped his hands together for attention and asked who would favour us with a Christmas tale, Emlyn McCarron growled: 'I suppose I've got something that bears telling. Tell it now or tell it never; God'll shut me up for good soon enough.'

In the years I had been coming to 249, I had never heard McCarron tell a story. And perhaps that's why I called the taxi so early, and why, when Stevens passed out eggnog to the six of us who had ventured out on that bellowing, frigid night, I felt so keenly excited. Nor was I the only one; I saw that same excitement on a good many other faces.

McCarron, old and dry and leathery, sat in the huge chair by the fire with the packet of powder in his gnarled hands. He tossed it in, and we watched the flames shift colours madly before returning to yellow again. Stevens passed among us with brandy, and we passed him his Christmas honorariums. Once, during that yearly ceremony, I heard the clink of change passing from the hand of the giver to the hand of the receiver; on another occasion, I had seen a one thousand dollar bill for a moment in the firelight. On both occasions the murmur of Stevens's voice had been exactly the same: low, considerate, and entirely correct. Ten years, more or less, had passed since I had first come to 249 with George Waterhouse, and while much had changed in the world outside, nothing had

breiteten sich unregelmäßig aus • Henker • Schlinge • hervorgetreten • Augapfel • eigentlich

in die Hände klatschte • beehren • knurrte • man erzählen könnte • für immer

austeilte • sich hinausgetraut • stürmisch • eisig • sehr

knotig • wechseln

Klirren • Kleingeld • ein anderes Mal

diskret

changed in here, and Stevens seemed not to have aged a month, or even a single day.

He moved back into the shadows, and for a moment there was a silence so perfect that we could hear the faint whistle of boiling sap escaping from the burning logs on the hearth. Emlyn McCarron was looking into the fire and we all followed his gaze. The flames seemed particularly wild that night. I felt almost hypnotized by the sight of the fire – as, I suppose, the cavemen who birthed us were once hypnotized by it as the wind walked and talked outside their cold northern caves.

At last, still looking into the fire, bent slightly forward so that his forearms rested on his thighs and his clasped hands hung in a knot between his knees, McCarron began to speak.

aged: älter geworden • whistle: Pfeifen • sap: Saft • hypnotized: hypnotisiert • cavemen: Höhlenmenschen • who birthed us: unsere Vorfahren waren • forearms: Unterarme • clasped: verschränkt

2: The Breathing Method

I am nearly eighty now, which means that I was born with the century. All my life I have been associated with a building which stands almost directly across from Madison Square Garden; this building, which looks like a great grey prison – something out of *A Tale of Two Cities* – is actually a hospital, as most of you know. It is Harriet White Memorial Hospital. The Harriet White after whom it was named was my father's first wife, and she got her practical experience in nursing when there were still actual sheep grazing on the Sheep's Meadow in Central Park. A statue of the lady herself (who would have been my stepmother, had she still been alive when I was born) stands on a pedestal in a pavilion before the building, and if any of you have seen it, you may have wondered how a woman with such a stern and uncompromising face could have found such a gentle occupation. The motto chiselled into the statue's base, once you get rid of the Latin folderol, is even less comforting: *There is no comfort without pain; thus we define salvation through suffering*. Cato, if you please … or if you don't please!

I was born inside that grey stone building on 20 March, 1900. I returned there as an intern in the year 1926. Twenty-six is old to be just starting out in the world of medicine, but I had done a more practical internship in France, at the end of World War I, trying to pack ruptured guts back into stomachs that had been blown wide open and dealing on the black market for morphine which was often tinctured and sometimes dangerous.

verbunden

(Roman von Charles Dickens) • benannt • Krankenpflege • die … weideten

Podest • Pavillon

eingemeißelt • Sockel • Firlefanz • so • Erlösung • wenn es Ihnen recht ist • Assistenzarzt

Praktikum • zerfetzt • Eingeweide • Morphium • gestreckt

Ärzte • unsentimental und praktisch • Medizinmänner • Versager • beständiger

As with the generation of physicians following World War II, we were a bedrock-practical lot of sawbones, and the records of the major medical schools show a remarkably small number of washouts in the years 1919 to 1928. We were older, more experienced, steadier. Were we also wiser? I don't know ... but we were certainly more cynical. There was none of this nonsense you read about in the popular medical novels, stuff about fainting or vomiting at one's first autopsy. Not after Belleau Wood, where mamma rats sometimes raised whole litters of ratlings in the gas-exploded intestines of the soldiers left to rot in no-man's land. We had gotten all our puking and passing out behind us.

sich übergeben • Rattenweibchen • Würfe • Eingeweiden • Kotzen • Ohnmächtigwerden • spielte eine ... Rolle • Assistenzarzt war

The Harriet White Memorial Hospital also figured largely in something that happened to me nine years after I had interned there – and this is the story I want to tell you gentlemen tonight. It is not a tale to be told at Christmas, you would say (although its final scene was played out on Christmas Eve), and yet, while it is certainly horrible, it also seems to express to me all the amazing power of our cursed, doomed species. In it I see the wonder of our will ... and also its horrible, tenebrous power.

unglücklich • zum Untergang verdammt • dunkel

Übung 19 Acht englische Begriffe sind in diesem Buchstabendickicht versteckt. Sie sind waagerecht, senkrecht oder diagonal angeordnet, aber jeweils von links nach rechts oder von rechts nach links sowie von oben nach unten oder umgekehrt!

Die deutschen Entsprechungen der Wörter lauten:

medizinisch	Geburt
Unfug	Grausamkeit
erstaunlich	Wispern
Mode	Motor

Birth itself, gentlemen, is a horrid thing to many; it is the fashion now that fathers should be present at the birth of their children, and while this fashion has served to inflict many men with a guilt which I feel they may not deserve (it is a guilt which some women use knowingly and with an almost prescient cruelty), it seems by and large to be a healthful, salubrious thing. Yet I have seen men leave the delivery room white and tottering and I have seen them swoon like girls, overcome by the cries and the blood. I remember one father who held up just fine … only to begin screaming hysterically as his perfectly healthy son pushed its way into the world. The infant's eyes were open, it gave the impression of looking around … and then its eyes settled on the father.

Birth is wonderful, gentlemen, but I have never found it beautiful – not by any stretch of the imagination. I believe it is too brutal to be beautiful. A woman's womb is like an engine. With conception, that engine is turned on. At first it barely idles … but as the creative cycle nears the climax of birth, that engine revs up and up and up. Its idling whisper becomes a steady running hum, and then a rumble, and finally a bellowing,

zuzufügen • absichtlich • weitblickend • gesund • bekömmlich • Kreißsaal • torkelnd • in Ohnmacht fallen • sich … hielt • Baby • fiel sein Blick auf • beim besten Willen nicht • Gebärmutter • Empfängnis • läuft leer • kommt auf Touren • Rumpeln

Y	T	L	E	U	R	C	N	F	E
X	V	V	X	U	M	J	V	A	N
M	E	D	I	C	A	L	E	S	I
K	A	Q	R	E	Z	S	Q	H	G
H	L	M	S	E	N	C	T	I	N
C	O	Z	A	E	P	R	T	O	E
U	Q	L	S	Z	I	S	Q	N	W
N	P	N	V	B	I	O	I	X	O
V	O	Y	P	W	Z	N	R	H	I
N	K	G	G	O	Y	H	G	L	W

frightening roar. Once that silent engine has been turned on, every mother-to-be understands that her life is in check. Either she will bring the baby forth and the engine will shut down again, or that engine will pound louder and harder and faster until it explodes, killing her in blood and pain.

Brüllen • werdende Mutter • auf dem Spiel steht • zur Welt • stampfen

This is a story of birth, gentlemen, on the eve of that birth we have celebrated for almost two thousand years.

Abend

I began practising medicine in 1929 – a bad year to begin anything. My grandfather was able to loan me a small sum of money, so I was luckier than many of my colleagues, but I still had to survive over the next four years mostly on my wits.

den Arztberuf auszuüben • leihen • mich schlau durchs Leben schlagen •

By 1935, things had improved a bit. I had developed a bedrock of steady patients and was getting quite a few outpatient referrals from White Memorial. In April of that year I saw a new patient, a young woman whom I will call Sandra Stansfield – that name is close enough to what her name really was. This was a young woman, white, who stated her age to be twenty-eight. After examining her, I guessed her true age to be between three and five years younger than that. She was blonde, slender, and tall for that time – about five feet eight inches. She was quite beautiful, but in an austere way that was almost forbidding. Her features were clear and regular, her eyes intelligent … and her mouth every bit as determined as the stone mouth of Harriet White on the statue in the pavilion across from Madison Square Garden. The name she put on her form was not Sandra Stansfield but Jane Smith. My examination subsequently showed her to be about two months gone in pregnancy. She wore no wedding ring.

Grundstock • Patienten, die von der Poliklinik … überwiesen wurden • angab • ich … untersucht hatte • schlank • (1,72 m) • herb • unnahbar • Gesichtszüge

später • schwanger •

After the preliminary exam – but before the results of the pregnancy test were in, my nurse, Ella Davidson,

Voruntersuchung

said: 'That girl yesterday? Jane Smith? If that isn't an assumed name, I never heard one.'
I agreed. Still, I rather admired her. She had not engaged in the usual shilly-shallying, toe-scuffing, blushing, tearful behaviour. She had been straightforward and businesslike. Even her alias had seemed more a matter of business than of shame. There had been no attempt to provide verisimilitude by creating a 'Betty Rucklehouse' or whomping up a 'Ternina DeVille'. *You require a name for your form*, she seemed to be saying, *because that is the law. So here is a name; but rather than trusting to the professional ethics of a man I don't know, I'll trust in myself. If you don't mind.*
Ella sniffed and passed a few remarks – 'modern girls' and 'bold as brass' – but she was a good woman, and I don't think she said those things except for the sake of form. She knew as well as I did that, whatever my new patient might be, she was no little trollop with hard eyes and round heels. No; 'Jane Smith' was merely an extremely serious, extremely determined young woman – if either of those things can be described by such a milquetoast adverb as 'merely'. It was an

falscher Name

sich … verhalten • unentschlossen • zögernd • direkt • sachlich • Deckname • Wahrhaftigkeit • erfinden • Berufsethik

rümpfte die Nase • frech wie Oskar • um die Form zu wahren • Hure • willensstark

zaghaft

Übung 20

Bilden Sie die Pluralformen der folgenden Wörter. Einige sind regelmäßig und einige unregelmäßig.

baby	________	caveman	________
life	________	closet	________
woman	________	mother-to-be	________
lens	________	foot	________
business	________	duffer	________

unpleasant situation (it used to be called 'getting in a scrape', as you gentlemen may remember; nowadays it seems that many young women use a scrape to get out of the scrape), and she meant to go through it with whatever grace and dignity she could manage.

A week after her initial appointment, she came in again. That was a peach of a day – one of the first real days of spring. The air was mild, the sky a soft, milky shade of blue, and there was a smell on the breeze – a warm, indefinable smell that seems to be nature's signal that she is entering her own birth cycle again. The sort of day when you wish you were miles from any responsibility, sitting opposite a lovely woman of your own – at Coney Island*, maybe, or on the Palisades* across the Hudson* with a picnic hamper on a checkered cloth and the lady in question wearing a great white cartwheel hat and a sleeveless gown as pretty as the day.

'Jane Smith's dress had sleeves, but it was still almost as pretty as the day; a smart white linen with brown edging. She wore brown pumps, white gloves, and a cloche hat that was slightly out of fashion – it was the first sign I saw that she was a far from rich woman.

in Schwulitäten kommen • Schaber • Anstand • Würde • erster Termin • herrlicher Tag
Ton • undefinierbar • beginnt • Geburtszyklus
Picknickkorb • kariert • rund • Gewand • so schön wie der Frühling selbst
Ränder • Kapotthut

info

Coney Island (Kanincheninsel) ist eine Halbinsel, die am südlichsten Zipfel von Long Island in New York liegt. Sie ist immer noch vor allem für ihre Vergnügungsparks bekannt. Ihre Blütezeit aber war zwischen 1867 und 1929. Um 1920 kamen über eine Million Besucher pro Tag dorthin.

Die Palisades (auch New Jersey Palisades oder Hudson Palisades genannt) sind eine Kette steiler Klippen am Ufer des Hudson River in New Jersey. Sie gehören jetzt zum Palisades Interstate Park, einem beliebten Wandergebiet. Von den Klippen aus kann man die beeindruckende New Yorker Skyline bewundern.

'You're pregnant,' I said. 'I don't believe you doubted it much, did you?'
If there are to be tears, I thought, they will come now.
'No,' she said with perfect composure. There was no more a sign of tears in her eyes than there were rain-clouds on the horizon that day. 'I'm very regular as a rule.'
There was a pause between us.
'When may I expect to deliver?' she asked then, with an almost soundless sigh. It was the sound a man or woman might make before bending over to pick up a heavy load.
'It will be a Christmas baby,' I said. '10 December is the date I'll give you, but it could be two weeks on either side of that.'
'All right.' She hesitated briefly, and then plunged ahead. 'Will you attend me? Even though I'm not married?'
'Yes,' I said. 'On one condition.'
She frowned, and in that moment her face was more like the face of Harriet White, my father's first wife, than ever. One would not think that the frown of a woman perhaps only twenty-three could be particular-

composure: Selbstbeherrschung • as a rule: normalerweise
deliver: entbinden • soundless: lautlos
load: Last
plunged ahead: fuhr fort • attend: behandeln
frowned: runzelte die Stirn

Übung 21

Ordnen Sie den folgenden Wörtern aus dem Text die passende deutsche Übersetzung zu.

unpleasant	Seufzer
nowadays	Leinen
responsibility	Bedingung
sleeve	unangenehm
linen	heutzutage
glove	zögern
sigh	Ärmel
to hesitate	Verantwortung
condition	Handschuh

beeindruckend

davon abhalten
• nichtssagend
• das Bedürfnis verspürte •
haselnussbraun
• Sie können weiter bar bezahlen • ausstellen • Quittungen •
anreden

ly formidable, but this one was. She was ready to leave, and the fact that she would have to go through this entire embarrassing process again with another doctor was not going to deter her.

'And what might that be?' she asked with perfect, colourless courtesy.

Now it was I who felt an urge to drop my eyes from her steady hazel ones, but I held her gaze. 'I insist upon knowing your real name. We can continue to do business on a cash basis if that is how you prefer it, and I can continue to have Mrs Davidson issue you receipts in the name of Jane Smith. But if we are going to travel through the next seven months or so together, I would like to be able to address you by the name to which you answer in all the rest of your life.'

behandelte •
gemacht •
ungeschickt •
würdelos

I finished this absurdly stiff little speech and watched her think it through. I was somehow quite sure she was going to stand up, thank me for my time, and leave forever. I was going to feel disappointed if that happened. I liked her. Even more, I liked the straightforward way she was handling a problem which would have reduced ninety women out of a hundred to inept and undignified liars, terrified by the living clock with-

Übung 22 Sind die folgenden Aussagen wahr oder falsch? Tragen Sie ein T für true oder ein F für false in die Kästchen ein.

1. ☐ The doctor cannot look the woman in the eye.
2. ☐ The doctor will ask Mrs Davidson to issue receipts in the woman's assumed name.
3. ☐ The doctor thinks the woman is handling the situation very well.
4. ☐ In the past, unmarried women who became pregnant were admired.
5. ☐ The woman decides to tell the doctor her real name.

in and so deeply ashamed of their situation that to make any reasonable plan for coping with it became impossible.

I suppose many young people today would find such a state of mind ludicrous, ugly, even hard to believe. People have become so eager to demonstrate their broad-mindedness that a pregnant woman who has no wedding ring is apt to be treated with twice the solicitude of one who does. You gentlemen will well remember when rectitude and hypocrisy were combined to make a situation that was viciously difficult for a woman who had gotten herself 'in a scrape'. In those days, a married pregnant woman was a radiant woman, sure of her position and proud of fulfilling what she considered to be the function God put her on earth for. An unmarried pregnant woman was a trollop in the eyes of the world and apt to be a trollop in her own eyes as well. They were, to use Ella Davidson's word, 'easy', and in that world and that time, easiness was not quickly forgiven. Such women crept away to have their babies in other towns or cities. Some took pills or jumped from buildings. Others went to butcher abortionists with dirty hands or tried to do the job themselves; in my time as a physician I have seen four women die of blood-loss before my eyes as the result of punctured wombs – in one case the puncturing was done by the jagged neck of a Dr Pepper bottle that had been tied to the handle of a whisk-broom. It *is* hard to believe now that such things happened, but they did, gentlemen. They did. It was, quite simply, the worst situation a healthy young woman could find herself in.

'All right,' she said at last. 'That's fair enough. My name is Sandra Stansfield.' And she held her hand out. Rather amazed, I took it and shook it. I'm rather glad Ella Davidson didn't see me do that. She would have made no comment, but the coffee would have been bitter for the next week.

beschämt • in den Griff zu bekommen • Haltung • lächerlich • Toleranz • wird oft • Zuwendung • Korrektheit • Heuchelei • verteufelt

strahlend

leicht zu haben • schlichen sich davon • Engelmacher

verbluten • perforiert • abgebrochen • Handfeger

Das kann ich verstehen.

Verwirrung • offen

She smiled – at my own expression of bemusement, I imagine – and looked at me frankly. 'I hope we can be friends, Dr McCarron. I need a friend just now. I'm quite frightened.'

'I can understand that, and I'll try to be your friend if I can, Miss Stansfield. Is there anything I can do for you now?'

billig • Notizblock • nahm ... in Schreibposition • Abtreiber

She opened her handbag and took out a dime-store pad and a pen. She opened the pad, poised the pen, and looked up at me. For one horrified instant I believed she was going to ask me for the name and address of an abortionist. Then she said: 'I'd like to know the best things to eat. For the baby, I mean.'

lachte laut auf • etwas verblüfft • geschäftsmäßig

I laughed out loud. She looked at me with some amazement.

'Forgive me – it's just that you seem so businesslike.'

'I suppose,' she said. 'This baby is part of my business now, isn't it, Dr McCarron?'

Faltblatt • Ernährung

'Yes. Of course it is. And I have a folder which I give to all my pregnant patients. It deals with diet and weight and drinking and smoking and lots of other things. Please don't laugh when you look at it. You'll hurt my feelings if you do, because I wrote it myself.'

mich kränken

Übung 23 Auf welches Wort im Text beziehen sich die folgenden Erklärungen?

1. To make your mouth wider in order to show that you are happy. __________
2. Carrying an unborn child in your body. __________
3. A long thin stick used for writing. __________
4. A person who is being treated by a doctor. __________
5. Contacts with people which are advantageous. __________
6. To focus intensively on one particular area of a subject of study. __________
7. A very short period of time. __________

And so I had – although it was really more of a pamphlet than a folder, and in time became my book. *A Practical Guide to Pregnancy and Delivery.* I was quite interested in obstetrics and gynaecology in those days – still am – although it was not a thing to specialize in back then unless you had plenty of uptown connections. Even if you did, it might take ten or fifteen years to establish a strong practice. Having hung out my shingle at a rather too-ripe age as a result of the war, I didn't feel I had the time to spare. I contented myself with the knowledge that I would see a great many happy expectant mothers and deliver a great many babies in the course of my general practice. And so I did; at last count I had delivered well over two thousand babies – enough to fill two hundred classrooms.

I kept up with the literature on having babies more smartly than I did on that applying to any other area of general practice. And because my opinions were strong, enthusiastic ones, I wrote my own pamphlet rather than just passing along the stale chestnuts so often foisted on young mothers then. I won't run through the whole catalogue of these chestnuts – we'd be here all night – but I'll mention a couple.

Merkblatt

Geburtshilfe • Gynäkologie • zu den besseren Kreisen • Praxis • da ich mich … selbstständig gemacht hatte

werdende

nach meiner letzten Zählung • blieb mit … auf dem Laufenden • gewissenhaft • altmodische Ratschläge • angedreht

Übung 24

Die folgende Zusammenfassung des Textes dieser Doppelseite enthält drei sachliche Fehler. Können Sie sie finden und korrigieren?

Miss Stansfield hopes that she and the doctor can be friends because this is a frightening time for her. She takes a pad and pencil from her handbag and asks him about her diet. Dr McCarron gives her a folder with advice on pregnancy which was written by a colleague. The doctor is interested in gynaecology but decided not to specialize in it. In his general practice he has still got to deliver over twelve thousand babies.

Expectant mothers were urged to stay off their feet as much as possible, and on no account were they to walk any sustained distance lest a miscarriage or 'birth damage' result. Now giving birth is an extremely strenuous piece of work, and such advice is like telling a football player to prepare for the big game by sitting around as much as possible so he won't tire himself out! Another sterling piece of advice, given by a good many doctors, was that moderately overweight mothers-to-be take up smoking … *smoking!* The rationale was perfectly expressed by an advertising slogan of the day: 'Have a Lucky instead of a sweet.' People who have the idea that when we entered the twentieth century we also entered an age of medical light and reason have no idea of how utterly crazy medicine could sometimes be. Perhaps it's just as well; their hair would turn white.

I gave Miss Stansfield my folder and she looked through it with complete attention for perhaps five minutes. I asked her permission to smoke my pipe and she gave it absently, without looking up. When she did look up at last, there was a small smile on her lips. 'Are you a radical, Dr McCarron?' she asked.

'Why do you say that? Because I advise that the expectant mother should walk her round of errands instead of riding in a smoky, jolting subway car?'

'"Pre-natal vitamins," whatever they are … swimming recommended … and breathing exercises! What breathing exercises?'

'That comes later on, and no – I'm not a radical. Far from it. What I am is five minutes overdue on my next patient.'

'Oh! I'm sorry.' She got to her feet quickly, tucking the thick folder into her purse.

'No need.'

She shrugged into her light coat, looking at me with those direct hazel eyes as she did so. 'No,' she said. 'Not

zu sitzen oder zu liegen • groß • damit nicht • Fehlgeburt • Entbinden • anstrengend • sich … erschöpft • fabelhaft • übergewichtig • zu … anfangen sollten • Begründung • Erleuchtung • ist das gut so • Erlaubnis • zerstreut • Besorgungen • rumpelnd • U-Bahn-Wagen • pränatal • Weit gefehlt. • … wartet schon fünf Minuten auf seinen Termin • und schob

a radical at all. I suspect you're actually quite … comfortable? Is that the word I want?'
'I hope it will serve,' I said. 'It's a word I like. If you speak to Mrs Davidson, she'll give you an appointment schedule. I'll want to see you again early next month.'
'Your Mrs Davidson doesn't approve of me.'
'Oh, I'm sure that's not true at all.' But I've never been a particularly good liar, and the warmth between us suddenly slipped away. I did not accompany her to the door of my consulting room. 'Miss Stansfield?'
She turned towards me, coolly enquiring.
'Do you intend to keep the baby?'
She considered me briefly and then smiled – a secret smile which I am convinced only pregnant women know. 'Oh yes,' she said, and let herself out.
By the end of that day I had treated identical twins for identical cases of poison ivy, lanced a boil, removed a hook of metal from a sheet-welder's eye, and had referred one of my oldest patients to White Memorial for what was surely cancer. I had forgotten all about Sandra Stansfield by then. Ella Davidson recalled her to my mind by saying:
'Perhaps she's not a chippie after all.'

umgänglich
Plan • hat etwas gegen
verflog • Sprechzimmer • fragend • betrachtete • überzeugt • machte sich die Tür auf • eineiig • Efeuvergiftung • aufgestochen • Furunkel • Schweißer • überwiesen • erinnerte mich an • Schlampe

Übung 25

Ersetzen Sie alle Substantive und Namen in den folgenden Sätzen durch die entsprechenden Personalpronomen.

Beispiel: The doctor gives Miss Stansfield a folder.
He gives her it.

1. Miss Stansfield puts the folder in her purse.

____

2. Expectant mothers are given advice by their doctors.

____

3. The doctor asks Miss Stansfield if she wants to keep the baby.

____

Akte • hilflos • Entrüstung • gemacht • Stempel

I looked up from my last patient's folder. I had been looking at it, feeling that useless disgust most doctors feel when they know they have been rendered completely helpless, and thinking I ought to have a rubber stamp made up for such files – only instead of saying ACCOUNT RECEIVABLE or PAID IN FULL or PATIENT MOVED, it would simply say DEATH-WARRANT. Perhaps with a skull and crossbones above, like those on bottles of poison.

ausstehend • Todesurteil • Totenkopf • gekreuzte Knochen

'Pardon me?'

'Your Miss Jane Smith. She did a most peculiar thing after her appointment this morning.' The set of Mrs Davidson's head and mouth made it clear that this was the sort of peculiar thing of which she approved.

Haltung

'And what was that?'

'When I gave her her appointment card, she asked me to tot up her expenses. *All* of her expenses. Delivery and hospital stay included.'

zusammenzuzählen • Kosten

That *was* a peculiar thing, all right. This was 1935, remember, and Miss Stansfield gave every impression of being a woman on her own. Was she well off, even comfortably off? I didn't think so. Her dress, shoes, and gloves had all been smart, but she had worn no

alleinstehend • reich • wohlhabend • schick

Übung 26 Bringen Sie die Buchstaben der Wörter in die richtige Reihenfolge. Alle Wörter sind auf dieser Doppelseite zu finden. Schreiben Sie sie auf und bilden Sie aus den Buchstaben, die in den Kästchen stehen, ein weiteres Wort von dieser Doppelseite. Die deutschen Übersetzungen der Wörter lauten:

1. Gift	**5.** Bargeld
2. seltsam	**6.** Quittung
3. Menschen	**7.** Handtasche
4. Frau	Extra-Wort = Termin

jewellery – not even costume jewellery. And then there was her hat, that decidedly out-of-date cloche. — Modeschmuck

'Did you do it?' I asked.

Mrs Davidson looked at me as though I might have lost my senses. *'Did I? Of course* I did! And she paid the entire amount. In cash.' — den Verstand verloren

The last, which apparently had surprised Mrs Davidson the most (in an extremely pleasant way, of course), surprised me not at all. One thing which the Jane Smiths of the world can't do is write cheques. — offensichtlich; ausschreiben •

'Took a bank-book out of her purse, opened it, and counted the money right out onto my desk,' Mrs Davidson was continuing. 'Then she put her receipt in where the cash had been, put the bank-book into her purse again, and said good day. Not half bad, when you think of the way we've had to chase some of these so-called "respectable" people to make them pay their bills!' — Sparbuch; gar nicht schlecht •; verfolgen •

I felt chagrined for some reason. I was not happy with the Stansfield woman for having done such a thing, with Mrs Davidson for being so pleased and complacent with the arrangement, and with myself, for some reason I couldn't define then and can't now. Something about it made me feel small. — ärgerte mich; selbstzufrieden; bestimmen

1. SOONIP _ _ _ _

2. CELRAPIU _ _ _ _ _ _

3. LEEPOP _ _ _ _ _

4. WOANM _ _ _

5. SAHC _ _ _ _

6. TEIRECP _ _ _ _ _

7. SUPRE _ _ _ _

Extra-Wort: _ _ _ _ _ _ _ _ _ _ _ T

'But she couldn't very well pay for a hospital stay now, could she?' I asked – it was a ridiculously small thing to seize on, but it was all I could find at that moment on which to express my pique and half-amused frustration. 'After all, none of us know how long she'll have to remain there. Or are you reading the crystal now, Ella?'

'I told her that very thing, and she asked what the average stay was following an uncomplicated birth. I told her three days. Wasn't that right, Dr MacCarron?'

I had to admit it was.

'She said that she would pay for three days, then, and if it was longer, she would pay the difference, and if –'

'– if it was shorter, we could issue her a refund,' I finished wearily. I thought: *Damn the woman, anyway!* – and then I laughed. She had guts. One couldn't deny that. All kinds of guts.

Mrs Davidson allowed herself a smile … and if I am ever tempted, now that I am in my dotage, to believe I know all there is to know about one of my fellow creatures, I try to remember that smile. Before that day I would have staked my life that I would never see Mrs Davidson, one of the most 'proper' women I have ever

to seize on: die ich aufgriff • pique: Ärger • crystal: Kristallkugel • that very thing: genau das • issue a refund: eine Rückvergütung vornehmen • wearily: resigniert • guts: Schneid • am in my dotage: langsam senil werde • fellow creatures: Mitmenschen • staked my life: darauf Gift genommen • proper: korrekt

Übung 27 Ergänzen Sie die fehlenden Buchstaben der englischen Begriffe.

1. A _ o _ _ _ t _ l is a building where sick people are treated.
2. If you buy something and decide afterwards that you don't want it after all, you can ask for a r _ _ u _ _.
3. If you have _ u _ _, then you are a brave person.
4. Another word for human beings in general is _ _ m _ _ i _ _.
5. To g _ _ g _ _ means to laugh quickly and quietly.
6. _ d _ i _ _ is something you give to someone who has a problem and doesn't know what to do.
7. G _ _ m _ _ _ is another general word for a piece of clothing.

known, smile fondly as she thought about a girl who was pregnant out of wedlock. — unverheiratet
'Guts? I don't know, Doctor. But she knows her own mind, that one. She certainly does.'

A month passed, and Miss Stansfield showed up promptly for her appointment, simply appearing out of that wide, amazing flow of humanity that was New York then and is New York now. She wore a fresh-looking blue dress to which she managed to communicate a feeling of originality, of one-of-a-kind-ness, despite the fact that it had been quite obviously picked from a rack of dozens just like it. Her pumps did not match it; they were the same brown ones in which I had seen her last time.

pünktlich • Menschenstrom

Einzigartigkeit

Stange

I checked her over carefully and found her normal in every way. I told her so and she was pleased. 'I found the pre-natal vitamins, Dr McCarron.' — untersuchte
'Did you? That's good.'
Her eyes sparkled impishly. 'The druggist advised me against them.'
'God save me from pestle-pounders,' I said, and she giggled against the heel of her palm – it was a childlike gesture, winning in its unselfconsciousness. 'I never met a druggist that wasn't a frustrated doctor. And a Republican. Pre-natal vitamins are new, so they're regarded with suspicion. Did you take his advice?'

spitzbübisch • Apotheker • Pillendreher • Handballen • Unbefangenheit • frustriert

Misstrauen

'No, I took yours. You're my doctor.'
'Thank you.'
'Not at all.' She looked at me straightforwardly, not giggling now. 'Dr McCarron, when will I begin to show?'
'Not until August, I should guess. September, if you choose garments which are … uh, voluminous.'

wird es auffallen, dass ich schwanger bin • wallend

'Thank you.' She picked up her purse but did not rise immediately to go. I thought that she wanted to talk … and didn't know where or how to begin.

'You're a working woman, I take it?'

She nodded. 'Yes. I work.'

'Might I ask where? If you'd rather I didn't –'

She laughed – a brittle, humourless laugh, as different from that giggle as day is from dark. 'In a department store. Where else does an unmarried woman work in the city? I sell perfume to fat ladies who rinse their hair and then have it done up in tiny finger-waves.'

'How long will you continue?'

'Until my delicate condition is noticed. I suppose then I'll be asked to leave. Lest I upset any of the fat ladies. The shock of being waited on by a pregnant woman with no wedding-band might cause their hair to straighten.'

Quite suddenly her eyes were bright with tears. Her lips began to tremble, and I groped for a handkerchief. But the tears didn't fall – not so much as a single one. Her eyes brimmed for a moment and then she blinked them back.

Her lips tightened … and then smoothed out. She simply decided she was not going to lose control of her emotions … and she did not. It was a remarkable thing to watch.

spröde • färben • Ringellöckchen • dass ich in anderen Umständen bin • beleidige • bedient • Ehering • glätten • fingerte nach • schwammen in Tränen • sie presste ihre Lippen zusammen • entspannten sie sich

Übung 28 Tragen Sie die gesuchten Begriffe in das Kreuzworträtsel ein.

1. An arrangement at a bank into which you can pay money.
2. To close one's eyes simultaneously for a moment.
3. To shake with tiredness or with fear.
4. A green-brown colour associated with a type of nut.
5. A drop of moisture produced by your eye when you are hurt or upset.
6. The power to make someone or something do what you want.
7. The absence of sound.
8. To use your money to pay for goods.
9. To move your head up and down in agreement.

'I'm sorry,' she said. 'You've been very kind to me. I won't repay your kindness with what would be a very common story.' She rose to go, and I rose with her.

'I'm not a bad listener,' I said, 'and I have some time. My next patient cancelled.'

'No,' she said.

'But there's something else.'

'Yes?'

'It's not my policy to make my patients – *any* of my patients – pay for services in advance of those services being rendered. I hope if you … that is, if you feel you'd like to … or have to …' I fumbled my way into silence.

'I've been in New York four years, Dr McCarron, and I'm thrifty by nature. After August – or September – I'll have to live on what's in my savings account until I can go back to work again. It's not a great amount and sometimes, during the nights, mostly, I become frightened.' She looked at me steadily with those wonderful hazel eyes.

'It seemed better to me – safer – to pay for the baby first. Ahead of everything. Because that is where the baby is in my thoughts, and because, later on, the temptation to spend that money might become very great.'

vergelten • gewöhnlich

hat abgesagt

ich mache es mir nicht zum Grundsatz

Ich fand die richtigen Worte nicht und schwieg. • sparsam • von … leben

Versuchung

1	U
2	N
3	M
4	A
5	R
6	R
7	I
8	E
9	D

'All right,' I said. 'But please remember that I see it as having been paid before accounts. If you need it, say so.'

'And bring out the dragon in Mrs Davidson again?' The light was back in her eyes. 'I don't think so. And now, Doctor –'

'You intend to work as long as possible? Absolutely as long as possible?'

'Yes. I have to. Why?'

'I think I'm going to frighten you a little before you go,' I said.

Her eyes widened slightly. 'Don't do that,' she said. 'I'm frightened enough already.'

'Which is exactly why I'm going to do it. Sit down again, Miss Stansfield.' And when she only stood there, I added: 'Please.' She sat. Reluctantly.

'You're in a unique and unenviable position,' I told her, leaning back against the examination table. 'You are dealing with the situation with remarkable grace.'

She began to speak, and I held up my hand to silence her.

'That's good. I salute you for it. But I would hate to see you hurt your baby in any way out of concern for your own financial security. I had a patient who, in spite of my strenuous advice to the contrary, continued packing herself into a girdle month after month, strapping it tighter and tighter as her pregnancy progressed. She was a vain, stupid, tiresome woman, and I don't believe she really wanted the baby anyway. I don't subscribe to many of these theories of the subconscious which everyone seems to discuss over the Mah-Jong* boards these days, but if I did, I would say that she – or some part of her – was trying to kill the baby.'

'And did she?' Her face was very still.

'No, not at all. But the baby was born retarded. It's very possible that the baby would have been born retarded anyway, and I'm not saying otherwise – we know next

im Voraus

Sie machte ziemlich große Augen.

Widerstrebend.

• nicht beneidenswert •

Untersuchungstisch

bewundere • weil Sie um … besorgt sind • Sicherheit • ausdrücklich • dagegen • sich in ein Korsett zwängte • das sie … schnürte • lästig • glaube … an • Unterbewusstsein •

geistig behindert •

kaum etwas

to nothing about what causes such things. But she *may* have caused it.'

'I take your point,' she said in a low voice. 'You don't want me to … to pack myself in so I can work another month or six weeks. I'll admit the thought had crossed my mind. So … thank you for the fright.'

This time I walked her to the door. I would have liked to ask her just how much – or how little – she had left in that savings book, and just how close to the edge she was. It was a question she would not answer; I knew that well enough. So I merely bade her goodbye and made a joke about her vitamins. She left. I found myself thinking about her at odd moments over the next month, and –

verstehe • dass mir der Gedanke schon gekommen ist • brachte … sie • Rand der Mittellosigkeit • verabschiedete … mich von ihr • ab und zu

Johanssen interrupted McCarron's story at this point. They were old friends, and I suppose that gave him the right to ask the question that had surely crossed all our minds.

'Did you love her, Emlyn? Is that what all this is about, this stuff about her eyes and smile and how you "thought of her at odd moments"?' I thought that McCarron might be annoyed at this interruption, but

Unterbrechung

info

Mah-Jong oder Mah-Jongg (auf Deutsch: Sperlingsspiel) ist ein altes chinesisches Spiel für vier Personen. Früher wurde behauptet, es hätte dieses Spiel schon vor 4000 Jahren gegeben. Tatsächlich aber entstand Mah-Jong wohl erst in der zweiten Hälfte des 19. Jahrhunderts in China. Das Spiel verbreitete sich rasch in China und Japan und wurde in den zwanziger und dreißiger Jahren des 20. Jahrhunderts zur Mode in den USA. Von den Regeln her kann man Mah-Jong als eine Variante des Kartenspiels Rommé beschreiben. Ein Mah-Jong-Spiel besteht aus 136, 144 oder 152 Ziegeln und wird in unzähligen Regelvarianten gespielt.

he was not. 'You have a right to ask the question,' he said, and paused, looking into the fire. It seemed that he might almost have fallen into a doze. Then a dry knot of wood exploded, sending sparks up the chimney in a swirl, and McCarron looked around, first at Johanssen and then at the rest of us.

'No. I didn't love her. The things I've said about her sound like the things a man who is falling in love would notice – her eyes, her dresses, her laugh.' He lit his pipe with a special boltlike pipe-lighter that he carried, drawing the flame until there was a bed of coals there. Then he snapped the bolt shut, dropped it into the pocket of his jacket, and blew out a plume of smoke that shifted slowly around his head in an aromatic membrane.

'I admired her. That was the long and short of it. And my admiration grew with each of her visits. I suppose some of you sense this as a story of love crossed by circumstance. Nothing could be further from the truth. Her story came out a bit at a time over the next half-year or so, and when you gentlemen hear it, I think you'll agree that it was every bit as common as she herself said it was. She had been drawn to the city

eingedöst • wirbelnd • zündete … an • bolzenartig • Pfeifenanzünder • zog an • der Tabak glühte • ließ … zuschnappen • Schwade • aromatisch • Membran • Das war alles. • halten das für • die an unglücklichen Umständen scheiterte • angezogen

Übung 29 Beantworten Sie die Fragen zum Text. Welche Lösung ist die richtige?

1. When McCarron doesn't answer the question it seems as if
a) he can't remember the answer.
b) he might have fallen asleep.
c) he doesn't know the answer.

2. McCarron lights his pipe with a lighter which resembles
a) a bottle.
b) a boat.
c) a bolt.

like a thousand other girls; she had come from a small town …

… in Iowa or Nebraska. Or possibly it was Minnesota – I don't really remember anymore. She had done a lot of high school dramatics and community theatre in her small town – good reviews in the local weekly written by a drama critic with an English degree from Cow and Silage Junior College – and she came to New York to try a career in acting.

She was practical even about that – as practical as an impractical ambition will allow one to be, anyway. She came to New York, she told me, because she didn't believe the unstated thesis of the movie magazines – that any girl who came to Hollywood could become a star, that she might be sipping a soda in Schwab's Drug Store one day and playing opposite Gable or MacMurray the next. She came to New York, she said, because she thought it might be easier to get her foot in the door there … and, I think, because the legitimate theatre interested her more than the talkies.

She got a job selling perfume in one of the big department stores and enrolled in acting classes. She was

in der Schule viel Theater gespielt • Laienspielgruppe • Kritiken • Zeitung • Theaterkritiker • Silofutter • als Schauspielerin • unbewiesen • Behauptung • Limo • die Gegenrolle zu • traditionell • Tonfilme • meldete sich zu … an

3. Which state did Miss Stansfield originally come from?

a) Minnesota.

b) Iowa.

c) McCarron can't remember.

4. Why did Miss Stansfield come to New York?

a) To try to become an actress.

b) To work at Schwab's Drug Store.

c) To work in one of the big department stores.

smart and terribly determined, this girl – her will was pure steel, through and through – but she was as human as anyone else. She was lonely, too. Lonely in a way that perhaps only single girls fresh from small midwestern towns know. Homesickness is not always a vague, nostalgic, almost beautiful emotion, although that is somehow the way we always seem to picture it in our mind. It can be a terribly keen blade, not just a sickness in metaphor but in fact as well. It can change the way one looks at the world; the faces one sees in the street look not just indifferent but ugly … perhaps even malignant. Homesickness is a real sickness – the ache of the uprooted plant.

Miss Stansfield, admirable as she may have been, determined as she may have been, was not immune to it. And the rest follows so naturally it needs no telling. There was a young man in her acting classes. The two of them went out several times. She did not love him, but she needed a friend. By the time she discovered he was not that and never would be, there had been two incidents. Sexual incidents. She discovered she was pregnant. She told the young man, who told her he would stand by her and 'do the decent thing'. A week

im Mittleren Westen • Heimweh • uns vorzustellen • scharf • Klinge • im übertragenen Sinne • gleichgültig • bösartig • aus dem Boden gerissen • bewundernswert • dagegen immun • man braucht sie nicht zu erzählen • Vorfälle • ihr beistehen • tun, was sich gehört

info

Die Lamaze-Methode wurde ursprünglich in Russland entwickelt und 1951 von dem französischen Geburtshelfer Fernand Lamaze übernommen. Sie ist heute in den USA geburtshilflicher Standard. Eine der Hauptthesen der Lamaze-Methode ist, dass die Angst vor den Wehen und der Verbrauch an Schmerzmitteln durch ein Verständnis für die Vorgänge deutlich verringert werden können. Deshalb wird diese Methode auch die „bewusste Geburt“ genannt. Durch gezielte Atem- und Entspannungsübungen wird dem Wehenschmerz entgegengewirkt. Bei jeder Wehe wird mit einer speziellen Atmung und dem Entspannen der Muskeln reagiert. Der Partner wird aktiv in den Geburtsablauf miteinbezogen.

later he was gone from his lodgings, leaving no forwarding address. That was when she came to me.

möbliertes Zimmer • Nachsendeadresse

During her fourth month, I introduced Miss Stansfield to the Breathing Method – what is today called the Lamaze Method*. In those days, you understand, Monsieur Lamaze was yet to be heard from.

'In those days' – the phrase has cropped up again and again, I notice. I apologize for it but am unable to help it – so much of what I have told you and will tell you happened as it did because it happened 'in those days.'

So … 'in those days', over forty-five years ago, a visit to the delivery rooms in any large American hospital would have sounded to you like a visit to a madhouse. Women weeping wildly, women screaming that they wished they were dead, women screaming that they could not bear such agony, women screaming for Christ to forgive them their sins, women screaming out strings of curses and gutter-words their husbands and fathers never would have believed they knew. All of this was quite the accepted thing, in spite of the fact that most of the world's women give birth in almost complete silence, aside from the grunting sounds of strain that we would associate with any piece of hard physical labour.

Doctors were responsible for some of this hysteria, I'm sorry to say. The stories the pregnant woman heard from friends and relatives who had already been through the birthing process also contributed to it. Believe me: if you are told that some experience is going to hurt, it *will* hurt. Most pain is in the mind, and when a woman absorbs the idea that the act of giving birth is excruciatingly painful – when she gets this information from her mother, her sisters, her married friends, *and* her physician – that woman has been mentally prepared to feel great agony. Even after only six years' practice, I had become used to seeing women

noch unbekannt • aufgetaucht • kann nichts dafür

Irrenanstalt • die … weinten

ertragen • Qual

Flüche • Kraftausdrücke • völlig normal

abgesehen von • ächzend • Anstrengung • Arbeit • Hysterie

trugen … dazu bei • Kopf • glaubt • qualvoll

zurechtzukommen • doppelt • Todesschatten • Angelegenheiten • Geburtshilfe • in der Medizin • machte sich die Mühe • bei diesem Stand der Dinge • (Name einer Nervenklinik) • Sitten • äußerst vage • auf vollen Touren war • gepackt

who were trying to cope with a twofold problem: not just the fact that they were pregnant and must plan for the new arrival, but also the fact – what most of them *saw* as a fact, anyway – *that they had entered the valley of the shadow of death*. Many were actually trying to put their affairs in coherent order so that if they *should* die, their husbands would be able to carry on without them.

This is neither the time nor place for a lesson on obstetrics, but you should know that for a long time before 'those days', the act of giving birth *was* extremely dangerous in the Western countries. A revolution in medical procedure, beginning around 1900, had made the process much safer, but an absurdly small number of doctors bothered to tell their expectant mothers that. God knows why. But in light of this, is it any wonder that most delivery rooms sounded like Ward Nine in Bellevue? Here are these poor women, their time come round at last, experiencing a process which has, because of the almost Victorian decorum of the times, been described to them only in the vaguest of terms; here are these women experiencing that engine of birth finally running at full power. They were seized

Übung 30 Setzen Sie die Verben in den folgenden Sätzen in die passende Verlaufsform wie im Beispiel.

Beispiel: The women tried to cope with a twofold problem.
The women **were trying** to cope with a twofold problem.

1. Many of the women have put their affairs in order.

____

2. They enter the valley of the shadow of death.

____

3. Miss Stansfield will have her baby at the hospital.

____

with an awe and wonder which they immediately interpreted as insupportable pain, and most of them felt that they would very shortly die a dog's death.
In the course of my reading on the subject of pregnancy, I discovered the principle of the silent birth and the idea of the Breathing Method. Screaming wastes energy which would be better used to expel the baby, it causes the women to hyperventilate, and hyperventilation puts the body on an emergency basis – adrenals running full blast, respiration and pulse-rate up – that is really unnecessary. The Breathing Method was supposed to help the mother focus her attention on the job at hand and to cope with pain by utilizing the body's own resources.
It was used widely at that time in India and Africa; in America, the Shoshone, Kiowa, and Micmac Indians all used it; the Eskimos have always used it; but, as you may guess, most Western doctors had little interest in it. One of my colleagues – an intelligent man – returned the typescript of my pregnancy pamphlet to me in the fall of 1931 with a red line drawn through the entire section on the Breathing Method. In the margin he had scribbled that if he wanted to know about 'nigger

Ehrfurcht • unerträglich • bald • elend zugrunde gehen würden • herauszupressen • hyperventilieren • Hyperventilation • Notlage • Nebennieren • arbeiten auf vollen Touren • Pulsfrequenz • sich auf … zu konzentrieren • vorliegend • indem sie … anwendete • Manuskript • Rand • gekritzelt • Neger

4. Dr McCarron has given her a lot of advice.

____

5. Miss Stansfield looks forward to the birth of her child.

____

6. Dr McCarron has read about the Breathing Method.

____

7. The mothers-to-be will soon experience great pain.

____

8. Many people around the world have used this method for centuries.

____

superstitions', he would stop by a newsstand and buy an issue of _Weird Tales*_!

Well, I didn't cut the section from the pamphlet as he had suggested, but I had mixed results with the method – that was the best one could say. There were women who used it with great success. There were others who seemed to grasp the idea perfectly in principle but who lost their discipline completely as soon as their contractions became deep and heavy. In most of those cases I found that the entire idea had been subverted and undermined by well-meaning friends and relatives who had never heard of such a thing and thus could not believe it would actually work.

The method was based on the idea that, while no two labours are ever the same in their specifics, all are pretty much alike in general. There are four stages: contractive labour, mid-labour, birth, and the expulsion of the afterbirth. Contractions are a complete hardening of the abdominal and pelvic-area muscles, and the expectant mother often finds them beginning in the sixth month. Many women pregnant for the first time expect something rather nasty, like bowel cramps, but I'm told it's much cleaner – a strongly physical sensation, which may deepen into a pain like a charley horse. A woman employing the Breathing Method began to breathe in a series of short, measured inhales and exhales when she felt a contraction coming on. Each breath was expelled in a puff, as if one were blowing a trumpet Dizzy Gillespie* fashion.

During mid-labour, when more painful contractions begin coming every fifteen minutes or so, the woman switched to long inhales followed by long exhales – it's the way a marathon runner breathes when he's starting his final kick. The harder the contraction, the longer the inhale-exhale. In my pamphlet, I called this stage 'riding the waves'. The final stage we need concern ourselves with here I called 'locomotive',

Kiosk
gestrichen • unterschiedlich
begreifen • Wehen
untergraben
Geburten • Eröffnungsperiode • Ausscheidung • Nachgeburt • Anspannung • Bauch- • Becken- • Darmkrämpfe • sich steigern • Muskelkater • gleichmäßig • Inhalationen • Exhalationen • Manier
ging zu … über
Endspurt
uns befassen

and Lamaze instructors today frequently call it the 'choo-choo' stage of breathing. Final labour is accompanied by pains which are most frequently described as deep and glassy. They are accompanied by an irresistible urge on the mother's part to push … to expel the baby.

This is the point, gentlemen, at which that wonderful, frightening engine reaches its absolute crescendo. The cervix is fully dilated. The baby has begun its short journey down the birth canal, and if you were to look directly between the mother's legs, you would be apt to see the baby's fontanell pulsing only inches from the open air. The mother using the Breathing Method now begins to take and let out short, sharp breaths between her lips, not filling her lungs, not hyperventilating, but almost panting in a perfectly controlled fashion. It really is the sound children make when they are imitating a steam-driven locomotive.

All of this has a salutary effect on the body – the mother's oxygen is kept high without putting her systems on an emergency basis, and she herself remains aware and alert, able to ask and answer questions, able to take instructions. But of course the *mental* results of

intensiv • Drang

Muttermund • geöffnet • können • Fontanelle

keuchend

dampfbetrieben • günstig • Sauerstoff • aufmerksam • Weisungen • geistig

info

Weird Tales ist ein US-amerikanisches Pulp-Magazin, in dem Science-Fiction- und Horror-Geschichten veröffentlicht werden. Die erste Ausgabe erschien im März 1923 in Chicago.

Dizzy Gillespie (1917–1993) war ein US-amerikanischer Jazztrompeter, Komponist, Sänger und Bandleader. Zusammen mit Charlie Parker hat er den Bebop-Stil erfunden. Später war er auch einer der ersten amerikanischen Jazzmusiker, der afrokubanische und lateinamerikanische Elemente in seine Kompositionen aufnahm. Er spielte eine Trompete mit nach oben gebogenem Schalltrichter und blies die Backen beim Spielen weit auf.

an … teilnahm • leitete • dass sie … beherrschte • geistige Einstellung • gefährdet • verwundbar • Fehlschläge • verunsichert • entsetzt sind • heidnisch • was das betraf • ausreden konnten • gerechterweise • sich zu etwas entschlossen hatte

the Breathing Method were even more important. The mother felt she was actively participating in the birth of her child – that she was in some part guiding the process. She felt on top of the experience … and on top of the pain.

You can understand that the whole process was utterly dependent on the patient's state of mind. The Breathing Method was uniquely vulnerable, uniquely delicate, and if I had a good many failures, I'd explain them this way – what a patient can be convinced of by her doctor she may be unconvinced of by relatives who raise their hands in horror when told of such a heathenish practice.

From this aspect, at least, Miss Stansfield was the ideal patient. She had neither friends nor relatives to talk her out of her belief in the Breathing Method (although, in all fairness, I must add that I doubt anyone ever talked her out of *anything* once she had made up her mind on the subject) once she came to believe in it. And she *did* come to believe in it.

'It's a little like self-hypnosis, isn't it?' she asked me the first time we really discussed it.

I agreed, delighted. 'Exactly! But you mustn't let that

Übung 31 Kreuzen Sie den Begriff an, der nicht zu den anderen passt.

1. Which of the following words has nothing to do with having a baby?

- ☐ labour
- ☐ birth
- ☐ cosmetics
- ☐ contractions

2. Which of the following words does not apply to Miss Stansfield?

- ☐ healthy
- ☐ slim
- ☐ young
- ☐ insane

make you think it's a trick, or that it will let you down when the going gets tough.'
'I don't think that at all. I'm very grateful to you. I'll practise assiduously, Dr McCarron.' She was the sort of woman the Breathing Method was invented for, and when she told me she would practise, she spoke nothing but the truth. I have never seen anyone embrace an idea with such enthusiasm ... but, of course, the Breathing Method was uniquely suited to her temperament. There are docile men and women in this world by the millions, and some of them are damn fine people. But there are others whose hands ache to hold the throttles of their own lives, and Miss Stansfield was one of those.
When I say she embraced the Breathing Method totally, I mean it ... and I think the story of her final day at the department store where she sold perfumes and cosmetics proves the point.
The end of her gainful employment finally came late in August. Miss Stansfield was a slim young woman in fine physical condition, and this was, of course, her first child. Any doctor will tell you that such a woman is apt not to 'show' for five, perhaps even six months ...

im Stich lassen • wenn es hart auf hart kommt • fleißig

annehmen • wie geschaffen für • fügsam • gut • die darauf brennen, ... zu bestimmen

beweist das • Erwerbstätigkeit

Verfassung

3. Which of the following does <u>not</u> describe the normal reactions of a patient's relatives to the Breathing Method?

- horror
- enthusiasm
- unhappiness
- rejection

4. Which of the following <u>cannot</u> be bought at a department store?

- clothes
- cosmetics
- perfumes
- cars

5. Which of the following words does <u>not</u> mean „Schmerzen"?

- patient
- agony
- hurt
- pain

and then, one day and all at once, *everything* will show.

Untersuchung • traurig — She came in for her monthly checkup on the first of September, laughed ruefully, and told me she had discovered the Breathing Method had another use.

'What's that?' I asked her.

furchtbar wütend • funkelten • Verrückte • zu schnaufen • zu pusten • — 'It's even better than counting to ten when you're mad as hell at someone,' she said. Those hazel eyes were dancing. 'Although people look at you as if you might be a lunatic when you start puffing and blowing.'

bereitwillig • plötzlich • Verwandlung • Tropen • Vorgesetzte — She told me the tale readily enough. She had gone to work as usual on the previous Monday, and all I can think is that the curiously abrupt transition from a slim young woman to an obviously pregnant young woman – and the transition really can be almost as sudden as day to dark in the tropics – had happened over the weekend. Or maybe her supervisor finally decided that her suspicions were no longer just suspicions.

betont kühl einmal — 'I'll want to see you in the office on your break,' this woman, a Mrs Kelly, said coldly. She had previously been quite friendly to Miss Stansfield. She had shown her pictures of her two children, both in high school, and they had exchanged recipes at one point. Mrs Kelly

Übung 32 Die folgenden Sätze enthalten jeweils einen grammatischen Fehler. Suchen und korrigieren Sie ihn.

1. Miss Stansfield growed angry with Mrs Kelly.
2. She kept her eyes fixed in Mrs Kelly.
3. He asked she what the other use for the Breathing Method was.
4. She was mad as hell on Mrs Kelly.
5. Mrs Kelly is always asking if she's meet a nice boy yet.
6. Miss Stansfield looks at Mrs Kelly curious.
7. Miss Stansfield refuses dropping her eyes.
8. She knows what reaction to expect when her secret comes off.

was always asking her if she had met 'a nice boy' yet. That kindliness and friendliness was gone now. And when she stepped into Mrs Kelly's office on her break, Miss Stansfield told me, she knew what to expect.

'You're in trouble,' this previously kind woman said curtly.

'Yes,' Miss Stansfield said. 'It's called that by some people.'

Mrs Kelly's cheeks had gone the colour of old brick. 'Don't you be smart with me, young woman,' she said. 'From the looks of your belly, you've been too smart by half already.'

I could see the two of them in my mind's eye as she told me the story – Miss Stansfield, her direct hazel eyes fixed on Mrs Kelly, perfectly composed, refusing to drop her eyes, or weep, or exhibit shame in any other way. I believe she had a much more practical conception of the trouble she was in than her supervisor did, with her two almost grown children and her respectable husband, who owned his own barber-shop and voted Republican.

'I must say you show remarkably little shame at the way you've deceived me!' Mrs Kelly burst out bitterly.

'I've never deceived you. No mention of my pregnancy has been made until today.' She looked at Mrs Kelly almost curiously. 'How can you say I have deceived you?'

'I took you home!' Mrs Kelly cried. 'I had you to dinner ... with my *sons*.' She looked at Miss Stansfield with utter loathing.

This is when Miss Stansfield began to grow angry. Angrier, she told me, than she had ever been in her life. She had not been unaware of the sort of reaction she could expect when the secret came out, but as any one of you gentlemen will attest, the difference between academic theory and practical application can sometimes be shockingly huge. Clutching her hands firmly together in her lap, Miss Stansfield said: 'If you are

Güte • betrat
schroff
Ziegelstein • frech • schon frech genug • im Geiste
beherrscht • zeigen • Vorstellung
Friseurladen
betrogen • stieß … hervor • ist … nicht erwähnt worden
habe … zum Abendessen eingeladen • Abscheu
bekannt wurde • bestätigen • Anwendung • die Hände verschränkend

verführen • gemeinste • schnellte zurück • Ohrfeige erhalten • ziegelrot • wich • grimmig • auf dem … herumstanden • Proben • riss … auf • sandfarben • Abfindungsbestätigung • Dirne • zu beschäftigen • verächtlich • zum Überschäumen • klappte herunter • ineinander verkrallt • Glieder

suggesting I made or ever would make any attempt to seduce your sons, that's the dirtiest, filthiest thing I've ever heard in my life.'

Mrs Kelly's head rocked back as if she had been slapped. That bricky colour drained from her cheeks, leaving only two small spots of hectic colour. The two women looked grimly at each other across a desk littered with perfume samples in a room that smelled vaguely of flowers. It was a moment, Miss Stansfield said, that seemed much longer than it actually could have been.

Then Mrs Kelly yanked open one of her drawers and brought out a buff-coloured cheque. A bright pink severance slip was attached to it. Showing her teeth, actually seeming to bite off each word, she said, 'With hundreds of decent girls looking for work in this city, I hardly think we need a strumpet such as yourself in our employ, dear.'

She told me it was that final, contemptuous 'dear' that brought all her anger to a sudden head. A moment later Mrs Kelly's jaw dropped and her eyes widened as Miss Stansfield, her hands locked together as tightly as links in a steel chain, so tightly she left bruises on

Übung 33 Welche Satzteile passen zusammen? Tragen Sie die entsprechenden Buchstaben in die Kästchen ein.

1. ☐ It wasn't a funny story, perhaps,
2. ☐ Mrs Kelly yanked open one of her drawers
3. ☐ I wasn't able to thank her, of course –
4. ☐ The two women looked grimly at each other
5. ☐ Mrs Kelly's head rocked back
6. ☐ I was going to do it;
7. ☐ Mrs Kelly's jaw dropped

herself (they were fading but still perfectly visible when I saw her on 1 September), began to 'locomotive' between her clenched teeth.
It wasn't a funny story, perhaps, but I burst out laughing at the image and Miss Stansfield joined me. Mrs Davidson looked in – to make sure we hadn't gotten into the nitrous oxide, perhaps – and then left again.
'It was all I could think to *do*,' Miss Stansfield said, still laughing and wiping her streaming eyes with her handkerchief. 'Because at that moment, I saw myself reaching out and simply sweeping those sample bottles of perfume – every one of them – off her desk and onto the floor, which was uncarpeted concrete. I didn't just *think* it, I *saw* it! I saw them crashing to the floor and filling the room with such a God-awful mixed stench that the fumigators would have to come.
'I was going to do it; nothing was going to stop me doing it. Then I began to breathe, and everything was all right. I was able to take the cheque, and the pink slip, and get up, and get out. I wasn't able to thank her, of course – I was still being a locomotive!'
We laughed again, and then she sobered.
'It's all passed off now, and I am even able to feel a little

verblassten • zusammengebissen • brach in Gelächter aus • lachte mit • Lachgas • tränend • teppichlos • wie sie krachend zu Boden fielen • ekelig • Gestank • Kammerjäger • wurde sie ernst • vorbei

a) as if she had been slapped.
b) I was still being a locomotive!
c) but I burst out laughing at the image.
d) nothing was going to stop me doing it.
e) across a desk littered with perfume samples.
f) and her eyes widened.
g) and brought out a buff-coloured cheque.

starrsinnig

sorry for her – or does that sound like a terribly stiff-necked thing to say?'

'Not at all. I think it's an admirable way to be able to feel.'

Abfindungsgeld

'May I show you something I bought with my severance pay, Dr McCarron?'

'Yes, if you like.'

Pfandhaus

She opened her purse and took out a small flat box. 'I bought it at a pawnshop,' she said. 'For two dollars. And it's the only time during this whole nightmare that I've felt ashamed and dirty. Isn't that strange?'

She opened the box and laid it on my desk so I could look inside. I wasn't surprised at what I saw. It was a plain gold wedding ring.

ordentlich • Pension • Mietdifferenz • die mir zusteht • Kaution

'I'll do what's necessary,' she said. 'I am staying in what Mrs Kelly would undoubtedly call "a respectable boarding house". My landlady has been kind and friendly … but Mrs Kelly was kind and friendly, too. I think she may ask me to leave at any time now, and I suspect that if I say anything about the rent-balance due me, or the damage deposit I paid when I moved in, she'll laugh in my face.'

'My dear young woman, that would be quite illegal. There are courts and lawyers to help you answer such –'

ruhig • sich besondere Mühe zu geben • helfen • so oder so • Kosten • ich hatte kein Recht

'The courts are men's clubs,' she said steadily, 'and not apt to go out of their way to befriend a woman in my position. Perhaps I could get my money back, perhaps not. Either way, the expense and the trouble and the … the unpleasantness … hardly seem worth the forty-seven dollars or so. I had no business mentioning it to you in the first place. It hasn't happened yet, and maybe it won't. But in any case, I intend to be practical from now on.'

She raised her head, and her eyes flashed at mine.

habe ein Auge auf … geworfen

'I've got my eye on a place down in the Village* – just in case. It's on the third floor, but it's clean, and it's five dollars a month cheaper than where I'm staying now.' She picked the ring out of the box. 'I wore this when the landlady showed me the room.'

She put it on the third finger of her left hand with a small moue of disgust of which I believe she was unaware. 'There. Now I'm Mrs Stansfield. My husband was a truck-driver who was killed on the Pittsburgh-New York run. Very sad. But I am no longer a little round-heels strumpet, and my child is no longer a bastard.'

She looked up at me, and the tears were in her eyes again. As I watched, one of them overspilled and rolled down her cheek.

'Please,' I said, distressed, and reached across the desk to take her hand. It was very, very cold. 'Don't, my dear.'

She turned her hand – it was the left – over in my hand and looked at the ring. She smiled, and that smile was as bitter as gall and vinegar, gentlemen. Another tear fell – just that one.

'When I hear cynics say that the days of magic and miracles are all behind us, Dr McCarron, I'll know they're deluded, won't I? When you can buy a ring in a pawnshop for a dollar and a half and that ring will

Ringfinger • Blick voller Abscheu • Lastwagenfahrer • Strecke • lose

lief über

betrübt

Galle

Zyniker • sie machen sich Illusionen

info

Greenwich Village ist ein Stadtteil von Manhattan in New York. Er erstreckt sich zwischen der 14. Straße und der Houston Street mit dem Broadway als Trennlinie zwischen zwei verschiedenen Bereichen mit den Namen East Village und West Village. Das Village ist ein Künstler- und Szeneviertel mit vielen Cafés, Bars, Restaurants, Clubs und Theatern. Es ist einer der Schwerpunkte der Lesben- und Schwulenszene. Mit seinen hübschen Ziegelsteinhäusern, kleinen Läden und den mit Bäumen gesäumten Straßen ist es auch ein beliebtes Wohnviertel.

Unehelichkeit • Unzüchtigkeit

instantly erase both bastardy and licentiousness, what else would you call that but magic? Cheap magic.'

'Miss Stansfield … Sandra, if I may … if you need help, if there's anything I can do –'

im Begriff

betrügerisch

She drew her hand away from me – if I had taken her right hand instead of her left, perhaps she would not have done. I did not love her, I've told you, but in that moment I could have loved her; I was on the verge of falling in love with her. Perhaps, if I'd taken her right hand instead of the one with that lying ring on it, and if she had allowed me to hold her hand only a little longer, until my own warmed it, perhaps then I should have.

hat sie mich davor bewahrt • wegen vorsätzlicher Sachbeschädigung • schmächtig • ängstlich • unsicher

'You're a good, kind man, and you've done a great deal for me and my baby … and your Breathing Method is a much better kind of magic than this awful ring. After all, it kept me from being jailed on charges of wilful destruction, didn't it?'

She left soon after that, and I went to the window to watch her move off down the street towards Madison Avenue. God, I admired her just then! She looked so slight, so young, and so obviously pregnant – but there was still nothing timid or tentative about her. She did

Übung 34

Acht englische Begriffe sind in diesem Buchstabendickicht versteckt. Sie sind waagerecht, senkrecht oder diagonal angeordnet, aber jeweils von links nach rechts <u>oder</u> von rechts nach links sowie von oben nach unten <u>oder</u> umgekehrt!

Die deutschen Entsprechungen der Wörter lauten:

Zauber	Podest
Streit	Bürgersteig
schrecklich	Atem
Stirn	Aufnahme

not scutter up the street; she walked as if she had every right to her place on the sidewalk.

She left my view and I turned back to my desk. As I did so, the framed photograph which hung on the wall next to my diploma caught my eye, and a terrible shudder worked through me. My skin – all of it, even the skin on my forehead and the backs of my hands – crawled up into cold knots of gooseflesh. The most suffocating fear of my entire life fell on me like a horrible shroud, and I found myself gasping for breath. It was a precognitive interlude, gentlemen. I do not take part in arguments about whether or not such things can occur; I know they can, because it has happened to me. Just that once, on that hot early September afternoon. I pray to God I never have another.

The photograph had been taken by my mother on the day I finished medical school. It showed me standing in front of White Memorial, hands behind my back, grinning like a kid who's just gotten a full-day pass to the rides at Palisades Park. To my left the statue of Harriet White can be seen, and although the photograph cuts her off at about mid-shin, the pedestal and that queerly heartless inscription – *There is no*

flitzte

ich verlor sie aus den Augen • fiel mein Blick auf • Schauder • überkam mich • überzog sich • Gänsehaut • erstickend • Schleier • Vorahnung

Tageskarte • Attraktionen • kurz über dem Fußgelenk

F B H H P L L S X H
A O F T U R J K P C
R O R F A E F A Z I
G R W E J E R E S G
U A A F H G R M R A
M S O L O E S B Z M
E Z R T X Z A L G V
N P O N I T T D X B
T H S I D E W A L K
P L A T S E D E P A

comfort without pain; thus we define salvation through suffering – could be clearly seen. It was at the foot of the statue of my grandfather's first wife, directly below that inscription, that Sandra Stansfield died not quite four months later in a senseless accident that occurred just as she arrived at the hospital to deliver her child.

sinnlos • zur Welt zu bringen

She exhibited some anxiety that fall that I would not be there to attend her during her labour – that I would be away for the Christmas holidays or not on call. She was partly afraid that she would be delivered by some doctor who would ignore her wish to use the Breathing Method and who would instead give her gas or a spinal block.

I assured her as best I could. I had no reason to leave the city, no family to visit over the holidays. My mother had died two years before, and there was no one else except a maiden aunt in California … and the train didn't agree with me, I told Miss Stansfield.

'Are you ever lonely?' she asked.

'Sometimes. Usually I keep too busy. Now, take this.' I jotted my home telephone number on a card and gave

Sorge • nicht in Bereitschaft • entbunden • Rückenmarkspritze • beruhigte • unverheiratet • mit dem Zug fuhr ich nicht gern • schrieb … auf

info

Jean Stratton-Porter (1863–1924) war eine US-amerikanische Schriftstellerin und Naturforscherin. Ihre berühmtesten Bücher, die Liebesromane Freckles (1904) und A Girl of the Limberlost (1909) spielen in den Sumpfgebieten Indianas, in denen die Autorin selbst lebte.

Pearl S. Buck (1892–1973) war eine US-amerikanische Schriftstellerin, die ihre Kindheit teilweise in China verbrachte. Ihre späteren Romane spielen überwiegend in China oder handeln von der Konfrontation zwischen den amerikanischen und chinesischen Kulturen. 1932 erhielt sie den Pulitzer-Preis für ihren Roman The Good Earth und 1938 den Nobelpreis für Literatur.

it to her. 'If you get the answering service when your labour begins, call me here.'

'Oh, no, I couldn't –'

'Do you want to use the Breathing Method, or do you want to get some sawbones who'll think you're mad and give you a capful of ether as soon as you start to "locomotive"?'

She smiled a little. 'All right. I'm convinced.'

But as the autumn progressed and the butchers on 3rd Avenue began advertising the per-pound price of their 'young and succulent Toms', it became clear that her mind was still not at rest. She had indeed been asked to leave the place where she had been living when I first met her, and had moved to the Village. But that, at least, had turned out quite well for her. She had even found work of a sort. A blind woman with a fairly comfortable income had hired her to come in twice a week, do some light housework, and then to read to her from the works of Jean Stratton-Porter* and Pearl Buck*. She had taken on that blooming, rosy look that most healthy women come to have during the final trimester of their pregnancies. But there was a shadow on her face. I would speak to her and she would be slow to answer … and once, when she didn't answer at all, I looked up from the notes I was making and saw her looking at the framed photograph next to my diploma with a strange, dreamy expression in her eyes. I felt a recurrence of that chill … and her response, which had nothing to do with my question, hardly made me feel easier.

'I have a feeling, Dr McCarron, sometimes quite a strong feeling, that I am doomed.'

Silly, melodramatic word! And yet, gentlemen, the response that rose to my own lips was this: *Yes; I feel that, too.* I bit it off, of course; a doctor who would say such a thing should immediately put his instruments

answering service: Telefonauftragsdienst
capful: Verschlusskappe • ether: Äther
succulent • Toms: saftig • Truthähne
turned out • comfortable • hired: sich als … erwiesen • gut • eingestellt
taken on • blooming • trimester: angenommen • blühend • Drittel
dreamy • recurrence • chill: abwesend • Wiederkehr • Schauder
doomed: verdammt
rose to my own lips • bit it off: mir auf der Zunge lag • sagte das nicht

and medical books up for sale and investigate his future in the plumbing or carpentry business. *(als Klempner oder Tischler)*

I told her that she was not the first pregnant woman to have such feelings, and would not be the last. I told her that the feeling was indeed so common that doctors knew it by the tongue-in-cheek *(ironisch)* name of The Valley of the Shadow Syndrome. I've already mentioned it tonight, I believe.

Miss Stansfield nodded with perfect seriousness *(Ernst)*, and I remember how young she looked that day, and how large her belly seemed. 'I know about that,' she said. 'I've felt it. But it's quite separate from this other feeling. This other feeling is like … like something looming up *(das sich abzeichnet)*. I can't describe it any better than that. It's silly, but I can't shake *(abschütteln)* it.'

'You must try,' I said. 'It isn't good for the –'

But she had drifted away from me *(hörte mir nicht zu)*. She was looking at the photograph again.

'Who is that?'

'Emlyn McCarron,' I said, trying to make a joke. It sounded extraordinarily feeble *(lahm)*. 'Back before the Civil War, when he was quite young.'

'No, I recognized you, of course,' she said. 'The woman.

Übung 35 Welches der angegebenen Wörter passt in die Lücke?

1. McCarron tells Miss Stansfield that she's not the first ___________ woman to feel doomed.

☐ beautiful ☐ unmarried ☐ pregnant

2. This doomed feeling is known amongst doctors as the ___________ of the Shadow Syndrome.

☐ Sensation ☐ Valley ☐ Sign

3. Miss Stansfield is unable to ___________ this feeling.

☐ remember ☐ forget ☐ shake

Who is the woman?'

'Her name is Harriet White,' I said, and thought: *And hers will be the first face you see when you arrive to deliver your child.* The chill came back – that dreadful drifting formless chill. *Her stone face.*

'And what does it say there at the base of the statue?' she asked, her eyes still dreamy, almost trancelike.

'I don't know,' I lied. 'My conversational Latin is not that good.'

That night I had the worst dream of my entire life – I woke up from it in utter terror, and if I had been married, I suppose I would have frightened my poor wife to death.

In the dream I opened the door to my consulting room and found Sandra Stansfield in there. She was wearing the brown pumps, the smart white linen dress with the brown edging, and the slightly out-of-date cloche hat. But the hat was between her breasts, because she was carrying her head in her arms. The white linen was stained and streaked with gore. Blood jetted from her neck and splattered the ceiling.

And then her eyes fluttered open – those wonderful hazel eyes – and they fixed on mine.

formlos • Sockel • wie in Trance • gesprochenes

zu Tode erschreckt

altmodisch • befleckt • schoss • bespritzte • zitterten und öffneten sich • richteten sich

4. McCarron thinks his joke sounds very ____________.

funny feeble clever

5. McCarron feels the __________ returning when he tells Miss Stansfield about Harriet White.

laughter chill memory

6. In his dream Miss Stansfield is carrying ________ head.

his the her

7. In his dream Miss Stansfield's linen dress is streaked __________ gore.

from for with

'Doomed,' the speaking head told me. 'Doomed. I'm doomed. There's no salvation without suffering. It's cheap magic, but it's all we have.'
That's when I woke up screaming.

errechnetes Geburtsdatum • sich … sehen zu lassen • mit Fassung • um vorzulesen • schmerzlicher Verlust • ins Auge sah • Bereitwilligkeit • ihr Interesse bekundet • werde davon Gebrauch machen • auf den Beinen • beurteile • dir die Tür weisen • hübsch verpackt • schob • und zog … auf • Krawattennadel

Her due date of 10 December came and went. I examined her on 17 December and suggested that, while the baby would almost certainly be born in 1935, I no longer expected the child to put in his or her appearance until after Christmas. Miss Stansfield accepted this with good grace. She seemed to have thrown off the shadow that had hung over her that fall. Mrs Gibbs, the blind woman who had hired her to read aloud and do light housework, was impressed with her – impressed enough to tell her friends about the brave young widow who, in spite of her recent bereavement and delicate condition, was facing her own future with such determined good cheer. Several of the blind woman's friends had expressed an interest in employing her following the birth of her child.
'I'll take them up on it, too,' she told me. 'For the baby. But only until I'm on my feet again, and able to find something steady. Sometimes I think the worst part of this – of everything that's happened – is that it's changed the way I look at people. Sometimes I think to myself, "How can you sleep at night, knowing that you've deceived that dear old thing?" and then I think, "If she knew, she'd show you the door, just like all the others." Either way, it's a lie, and I feel the weight of it on my heart sometimes.'
Before she left that day, she took a small, gaily wrapped package from her purse and slid it shyly across the desk to me. 'Merry Christmas, Dr McCarron.'
'You shouldn't have,' I said, sliding open a drawer and taking out a package of my own. 'But since I did, too –'
She looked at me for a moment, surprised … and then we laughed together. She had gotten me a silver tie-

clasp with the medical symbol on it. I had gotten her an album in which to keep photographs of her baby. I still have the tie-clasp. What happened to the album, I cannot say.

I saw her to the door, and as we reached it, she turned to me, put her hands on my shoulders, stood on tiptoe, and kissed me on the mouth. Her lips were cool and firm. It was not a passionate kiss, gentlemen, but neither was it the sort of kiss you might expect from a sister or an aunt.

stellte sich auf die Zehenspitzen • leidenschaftlich

'Thank you again, Dr McCarron,' she said a little breathlessly. The colour was high in her cheeks and her hazel eyes glowed lustrously. 'Thank you for so much.'

atemlos • ihre Wangen waren rot • hell •

I laughed – a little uneasily. 'You speak as if we'll never meet again, Sandra.' It was, I believe, the second and last time I ever used her Christian name.

unsicher

Vorname

'Oh, we'll meet again,' she said. 'I don't doubt it a bit.'

And she was right – although neither of us could have foreseen the dreadful circumstances of that last meeting.

vorhergesehen

Übung 36

Bringen Sie die Aussagen in die richtige chronologische Reihenfolge und tragen Sie die entsprechenden Nummern in die Kästchen ein.

1 McCarron wakes up screaming from his nightmare.
Miss Stansfield says she's sure they'll meet again.
Miss Stansfield gives McCarron a Christmas present.
McCarron examines Miss Stansfield on 17 December.
Miss Stansfield stands on tiptoe to kiss McCarron.
Miss Stansfield says she's going to accept the offers of work from the blind woman's friends.
McCarron sees Miss Stansfield to the door.

Sandra Stansfield's labour began on Christmas Eve, at just past six p.m. By that time, the snow which had fallen all that day had changed to sleet. And by the time Miss Stansfield entered mid-labour, not quite two hours later, the city streets were a dangerous glaze of ice.

Mrs Gibbs, the blind woman, had a large and spacious first-floor apartment, and at 6.30 p.m. Miss Stansfield worked her way carefully downstairs, knocked at her door, was admitted, and asked if she might use the telephone to call a cab.

'Is it the baby, dear?' Mrs Gibbs asked, fluttering already.

'Yes. The labour's only begun, but I can't chance the weather. It will take a cab a long time.'

She made that call and then called me. At that time, 6.40, the pains were coming at intervals of about twenty-five minutes. She repeated to me that she had begun everything early because of the foul weather. 'I'd rather not have my child in the back of a Yellow,' she said. She sounded extraordinarily calm.

The cab was late and Miss Stansfield's labour was progressing more rapidly than I would have predicted –

sleet: Schneeregen • entered mid-labour: die Austreibungsperiode erreichte • glaze of ice: Glatteis • spacious: geräumig • admitted: hereingebeten • fluttering: aufgeregt • chance: riskieren • intervals: Abständen • foul: schlecht • Yellow: gelbes Taxi • progressing: schritten … fort • predicted: erwartet

Übung 37 Bringen Sie die Buchstaben der Wörter in die richtige Reihenfolge. Alle Wörter sind auf dieser Doppelseite zu finden. Schreiben Sie sie auf und bilden Sie aus den Buchstaben, die in den Kästchen stehen, ein weiteres Wort von dieser Doppelseite. Die deutschen Übersetzungen der Wörter lauten:

1. Schneeregen
2. gefährlich
3. ruhig
4. Unfall
5. Spiegel
6. geräumig
7. gesund
Extra-Wort = Kreuzung

but as I have said, no two labours are alike in their specifics. The driver, seeing that his fare was about to have a baby, helped her down the slick steps, constantly adjuring her to 'be careful, lady'. Miss Stansfield only nodded, preoccupied with her deep inhale-exhales as a fresh contraction seized her. Sleet ticked off streetlights and the roofs of cars; it melted in large, magnifying drops on the taxi's yellow dome-light. Miss Gibbs told me later that the young cab driver was more nervous than her 'poor, dear Sandra', and that was probably a contributing cause to the accident.

Another was almost certainly the Breathing Method itself.

The driver threaded his hack through the slippery streets, working his way slowly past the fender-benders and inching through the clogged intersections, slowly closing on the hospital. He was not seriously injured in the accident, and I talked to him in the hospital. He said the sound of the steady deep breathing coming from the back seat made him nervous; he kept looking in the rear view mirror to see if she was 'dine or sumpin''. He said he would have felt less nervous if she had let out a few healthy bellows, the way a woman in labour was

Einzelheiten • Fahrgast • schlüpfrig • und mahnte • beschäftigt • überkam • tanzte auf • vergrößernd • Leuchtbuchstaben • beitragend

Droschke • Bagatellunfälle • kroch • verstopft • näherte sich • schwer

Rückspiegel • starb oder so etwas • Schreie

1. TESLE _ _ _
2. ODEGASUNR _ _ _ _ _ _ _ _
3. MCLA _ _ _
4. DACTICNE _ _ _ _ _ _
5. RRMORI _ _ _ _
6. AIPSSUCO _ _ _ _ _ _ _
7. YALHEHT _ _ _ _ _

Extra-Wort: _ _ _ _ _ _ _ _ _ _ _ N

supposed to do. He asked her once or twice if she was feeling all right and she only nodded, continuing to 'ride the waves' in deep inhales and exhales.

Anfang — Two or three blocks from the hospital, she must have felt the onset of labour's final stage. An hour had passed since she had entered the cab – the traffic was chaotisch — that snarled – but this was still an extraordinarily fast labour for a woman having her first baby. The driver noticed the change in the way she was breathing. 'She hecheln — started pantin' like a dog on a hot day, Doc,' he told me. She had begun to 'locomotive'.

Lücke • vorbeifahrende Fahrzeuge • Tussi • loszuwerden • Gaspedal • schoss • Haftung • fiel ... zusammen • unterschätzt • Straßenverhältnisse • eingeliefert

At almost the same time the cabbie saw a hole open up in the crawling cross-traffic and shot through it. The way to White Memorial was now open. It was less than three blocks ahead. 'I could see the statue of that broad,' he said. Eager to be rid of his panting, pregnant passenger, he stepped down on the gas again and the cab leaped forward, wheels spinning over the ice with little or no traction.

I had walked to the hospital, and my arrival coincided with the cab's arrival only because I had underestimated just how bad driving conditions had become. I believed I would find her upstairs, a legally admitted

Übung 38 Welche Wörter gehören zusammen? Verbinden Sie sie mit einer Linie.

upside	stage
emergency	coloured
brake	bag
blood	down
driving	traffic
final	wing
cross	pedal
severed	conditions
black	head

patient with all her papers signed, her prep completed, working her way steadily through her mid-labour. I was mounting the steps when I saw the sudden sharp convergence of two sets of headlights reflected from the patch of ice where the janitors hadn't yet spread cinders. I turned just in time to see it happen.

An ambulance was nosing its way out of the Emergency Wing rampway as Miss Stansfield's cab came across the Square and towards the hospital. The cab was simply going too fast to stop. The cabbie panicked and stamped down on the brake-pedal rather than pumping it. The cab slid, then began to turn broadside. The pulsing dome-light of the ambulance threw moving stripes and blotches of blood-coloured light over the scene, and, freakishly, one of these illuminated the face of Sandra Stansfield. For that one moment it was the face in my dream, the same bloody, open-eyed face that I had seen on her severed head.

I cried out her name, took two steps down, slipped, and fell sprawling. I cracked my elbow a paralyzing blow but somehow managed to hold on to my black bag. I saw the rest of what happened from where I lay, head ringing, elbow smarting.

The ambulance braked, and it also began to fishtail. Its rear end struck the base of the statue. The loading doors flew open. A stretcher, mercifully empty, shot out like a tongue and then crashed upside down in the street with its wheels spinning. A young woman on the sidewalk screamed as the two vehicles approached each other and tried to run. Her feet went out from under her after two strides and she fell on her stomach. Her purse flew out of her hand and shot down the icy sidewalk like a weight in a pinball bowling game.

The cab swung all the way around, now travelling backwards, and I could see the cabbie clearly. He was spinning his wheel madly, like a kid in a Dodgem Car. The ambulance rebounded from Mrs White's statue at

Vorbereitung

stieg ... hinauf • Annäherung • Hausmeister • Asche • verließ langsam • Rampe

trat heftig auf • schleuderte • um die eigene Achse • Flecken • seltsamerweise

abgetrennt • rutschte aus • fiel der Länge nach hin • stieß mir sehr heftig den Ellenbogen • schmerzend • schleudern • Hintertüren • Trage

rutschten unter ihr weg

Flipperspiel

Autoskooter • prallte ... ab

an angle … and smashed broadside into the cab. The taxi spun around once in a tight circle and was slammed against the base of the statue with fearful force. Its yellow light, the letters ON RADIO CALL still flashing, exploded like a bomb. The left side of the cab crumpled like tissue-paper. A moment later I saw that it was not just the left side; the cab had struck an angle of the pedestal hard enough to tear it in two. Glass sprayed onto the slick ice like diamonds. And my patient was thrown through the rear right-side window of the dismembered cab like a rag-doll.

I was on my feet again without even knowing it. I raced down the icy steps, slipped again, caught at the railing, and kept on. I was only aware of Miss Stansfield lying in the uncertain shadow cast by that hideous statue of Harriet White, some twenty feet from where the ambulance had come to rest on its side, flasher still strobing the night with red. There was something terribly wrong with that figure, but I honestly don't believe I knew what it was until my foot struck something with a heavy enough thud to almost send me sprawling again. The thing I'd kicked skittered away – like the young woman's purse, it slid rather than rolled. It skit-

prallte gegen • geknallt • ungeheuer • Wucht • blinkte • zerknitterte • Seidenpapier

sprühte • zertrümmert • Stoffpuppe

Geländer

geworfen

zum Stillstand gekommen • Licht • erleuchtete • dumpfer Aufschlag • rutschte

Übung 39

Die folgenden Wörter bedeuten das Gegenteil von Wörtern auf dieser Doppelseite. Tragen Sie die gesuchten Wörter ein.

1. top ______________
2. front ______________
3. beautiful ______________
4. weakness ______________
5. upper ______________
6. stillness ______________
7. stale ______________
8. sane ______________
9. to push ______________

tered away and it was only the fall of hair – blood-streaked but still recognizably blonde, speckled with bits of glass – that made me realize what it was. She had been decapitated in the accident. What I had kicked into the frozen gutter was her head.

Moving in total numb shock, now I reached her body and turned it over. I think I tried to scream as soon as I had done it, as soon as I saw. If I did, no sound came out; I could not make a sound. The woman was still breathing, you see, gentlemen. Her chest was heaving up and down in quick, light, shallow breaths. Ice pattered down on her open coat and her blood-drenched dress. And I could hear a high, thin whistling noise. It waxed and waned like a teakettle which can't quite reach the boil. It was air being pulled into her severed windpipe and then exhaled again; the little screams of air through the crude reed of the vocal chords which no longer had a mouth to shape their sounds.

I wanted to run but I had no strength; I fell on my knees beside her on the ice, one hand cupped to my mouth. A moment later I was aware of fresh blood seeping through the lower part of her dress – and of movement there. I became suddenly, frenziedly convinced that there was still a chance to save the baby.

'Cheap magic!' I roared into the sleet, and I believe that as I yanked her dress up to her waist I began laughing. I believe I was mad. Her body was warm. I remember that. I remember the way it heaved with her breathing. One of the ambulance attendants came up, weaving like a drunk, one hand clapped to the side of his head. Blood trickled through his fingers.

'Cheap magic!' I screamed again, still laughing, still groping. My hands had found her fully dilated.

The attendant stared down at Sandra Stansfield's headless body with wide eyes. I don't know if he realized the corpse was still somehow breathing or not. Perhaps he thought it was merely a thing of the nerves – a kind of

gesprenkelt
geköpft • Gosse • betäubt
hob und senkte sich • flach • prasselte • blutgetränkt • schwankte in der Lautstärke • abgerissen • Luftröhre • grob • Rohrblatt • Stimmbänder • gehalten
das … durchsickerte • wild
brüllte • hochschlug
Sanitäter • schwankte • hielt er an • tröpfelte • tastend
Leiche

final reflex action. If he did think such a thing, he could not have been driving an ambulance long. Chickens may walk around for a while with their heads cut off, but people only twitch once or twice … if that.

'Stop staring at her and get me a blanket,' I snapped at him.

zucken • wenn überhaupt • fuhr … an

He wandered away, but not back towards the ambulance. He was pointed more or less towards Times Square. He simply walked off into the sleety night. I have no idea what became of him. I turned back to the dead woman who was somehow not dead, hesitated a moment, and then stripped off my overcoat. Then I lifted her hips so I could get it under her. Still I heard that whistle of breath as her headless body did 'locomotive' breathing. I sometimes hear it still, gentlemen. In my dreams.

ging … in Richtung auf • graupelig

zog mir … aus

Please understand that all of this had happened in an extremely short time – it seemed longer to me, but only because my perceptions had been heightened to a feverish pitch. People were only beginning to run out of the hospital to see what had happened, and behind me a woman shrieked as she saw the severed head lying by the edge of the street.

Wahrnehmungen • sich … verstärkt • fieberhaft • kreischte

I yanked open my black bag, thanking God I hadn't lost it in my fall, and pulled out a short scalpel. I opened it, cut through her underwear, and pulled it off. Now the ambulance driver approached – he came to within fifteen feet of us and then stopped dead. I glanced over at him, still wanting that blanket. I wasn't going to get it from him, I saw; he was staring down at the breathing body, his eyes widening until it seemed they must slip from their orbits and simply dangle from their optic nerves like grotesque seeing yo-yos. Then he dropped to his knees and raised his clasped hands. He meant to pray, I am quite sure of that. The attendant might not have known he was seeing an impossibility, but this fellow did. The next moment he had fainted dead away.

Skalpell

blieb wie angewurzelt stehen

Höhlen • herunterbaumeln • Sehnerven

bewusstlos in sich zusammengesunken

I had packed forceps in my bag that night; I don't know why. I hadn't used such things in three years, not since I had seen a doctor I will not name punch through a newborn's temple and into the child's brain with one of those infernal gadgets. The child died instantly. The corpse was 'lost' and what went on the death certificate was *stillborn*. But, for whatever reason, I had them.
Miss Stansfield's body tightened down, her belly clenching, turning from flesh to stone. And the baby crowned. I saw the crown for just a moment, bloody and membranous and pulsing. *Pulsing.* It was alive, at least then. Definitely alive.
Stone became flesh again. The crown slipped back out of sight. And a voice behind me said: 'What can I do, Doctor?'
It was a middle-aged nurse, the sort of woman who is so often the backbone of our profession. Her face was as pale as milk, and while there was terror and a kind of superstitious awe on her face as she looked down at that weirdly breathing body, there was none of that dazed shock which would have made her difficult and dangerous to work with. 'You can get me a blanket, stat,' I said curtly. 'We've still got a chance, I think.'

Zange

durchstechen • Schläfe • teuflisch • Instrumente • tot geboren • straffte sich • Bauchmuskeln • zogen sich zusammen • der Kopf des Babys wurde sichtbar • Kopf

Rückgrat

abergläubisch

betäubt

sofort

Übung 40

Bringen Sie die Buchstaben der Wörter in Klammern in die richtige Reihenfolge und vervollständigen Sie die folgenden Sätze.

1. McCarron tells the ambulance attendant to bring him a ___________ (kbnaetl).
2. McCarron strips off his ___________ (aetrvcoo).
3. McCarron opens his black bag and takes out a ___________ (llaepcs).
4. When McCarron sees the crown he knows that the baby is ___________ (elaiv).
5. McCarron is helped by a middle-aged ________ (seurn).

Behind her I saw perhaps two dozen people from the hospital standing on the steps, not wanting to come any closer. How much or how little did they see? I have no way of knowing for sure. All I know is that I was avoided for days afterwards (and forever by some of them), and no one, including this nurse, ever spoke to me of it.

She now turned and started back towards the hospital. 'Nurse!' I called. 'No time for that. Get one from the ambulance. This baby is coming *now.*'

She changed course, slipping and sliding through the slush in her white crêpe-soled shoes. I turned back to Miss Stansfield.

Rather than slowing down, the locomotive breathing had actually begun to speed up … and then her body turned hard again, locked and straining. The baby crowned again. I waited for it to slip back but it did not; it simply kept coming. There was no need for the forceps after all. The baby all but *flew* into my hands. I saw the sleet ticking off its naked, bloody body – for it *was* a boy, his sex unmistakable. I saw steam rising from it as the black, icy night snatched away the last of its mother's heat. Its blood-grimed fists waved feebly; it uttered a thin, wailing cry.

'Nurse!' I bawled, *'move your ass, you bitch!'* It was perhaps inexcusable language, but for a moment I felt I was back in France, that in a few moments the shells would begin to whistle overhead with a sound like that remorselessly ticking sleet; the machine-guns would begin their hellish stutter; the Germans would begin to materialize out of the murk, running and slipping and cursing and dying in the mud and smoke. *Cheap magic*, I thought, seeing the bodies twist and turn and fall. *But you're right, Sandra, it's all we have.* It was the closest I have ever come to losing my mind, gentlemen.

'NURSE, FOR GOD'S SAKE!'

ging auf … zu
Schneematsch • Kreppsohlen- • schneller zu werden • stramm • gespannt
fast
Geschlecht • aufstieg • verschlang • blutverschmiert • stieß … aus
• brüllte • mach schnell • Schlampe • unverzeihlich • Granaten • unerbittlich • Geknatter • aufzutauchen • Finsternis • Verstand

The baby wailed again – such a tiny, lost sound! – and then it wailed no more. The steam rising from its skin had thinned to ribbons. I put my mouth against its face, smelling blood and the bland, damp aroma of placenta. I breathed into its mouth and heard the jerky susurrus of its breathing resume. Then the nurse was there, the blanket in her arms. I held out my hand for it.

wimmerte • kam jetzt nur in dünnen Fetzen • fade • Plazenta • zuckend • Säuseln • wieder anfangen

She started to give it to me, and then held it back. 'Doctor, what … what if it's a monster? Some kind of monster?'

'Give me that blanket,' I said. 'Give it to me now, Sarge, before I kick your fucking asshole right up your fucking shoulderblades.'

Sergeant • Arschloch • Schulterblätter

'Yes, doctor,' she said with perfect calmness (we must bless the women, gentlemen, who so often understand simply by not trying to), and gave me the blanket. I wrapped the child and gave it to her.

segnen

'If you drop him, Sarge, you'll be eating those stripes.'

wickelte … ein • Ärmelstreifen

'Yes, doctor.'

'It's cheap fucking magic, Sarge, but it's all God left us with.'

'Yes, doctor.'

Übung 41

Ordnen Sie den folgenden Wörtern aus dem Text die passende deutsche Übersetzung zu.

afterwards	Wolldecke
naked	Dampf
unmistakable	Schlamm
steam	nachher
heat	unverkennbar
feebly	nackt
mud	Wärme
blanket	vollkommen
perfect	schwach

I watched her half-walk, half-run [teils ging, teils lief] back to the hospital with the child and watched the crowd on the steps part for her. Then I rose to my feet and backed away [trat … zurück] from the body. Its breathing, like the baby's, hitched [kam wieder] and caught [stockte] … stopped … hitched again … stopped …

I began to back away from it. My foot struck something. I turned. It was her head. And obeying some directive [Weisung] from outside of me, I dropped to one knee and turned the head over. The eyes were open – those direct [gerade] hazel eyes that had always been full of such life and such determination. They were full of determination still. Gentlemen, *she was seeing me*.

Her teeth were clenched, her lips slightly parted [geöffnet]. I heard the breath slipping rapidly back and forth between those lips and through those teeth as she "locomotived". Her eyes moved; they rolled slightly to the left in their sockets [Höhlen] so as to see me better. Her lips parted. They mouthed [formten] four words: *Thank you, Doctor McCarron.* And I *heard* them, gentlemen, but not from her mouth. They came from twenty feet away. From her vocal cords. And because her tongue and lips and teeth, all of which we use to shape our words, were here, they came out only in unformed modulations of [unartikulierte Laute]

Übung 42 In jeder Zeile steht ein Wort, das nicht zu den anderen passt. Streichen Sie es durch.

1. ambulance – socket – stretcher – hospital
2. foot – shoe – head – mouth
3. statue – lighter – pipe – tobacco
4. tongue – lips – teeth – toe
5. nurse – intern – cabbie – doctor
6. sunshine – sleet – snow – slush

sound. But there were seven of them, seven distinct sounds, just as there are seven syllables in that phrase, *Thank you, Doctor McCarron.*

einzeln • Silben

'You're welcome, Miss Stansfield,' I said. 'It's a boy.'

Her lips moved again, and from behind me, thin, ghostly, came the sound *hoyyyyyy* –

gespenstisch •

Her eyes lost their focus and their determination. They seemed now to look at something beyond me, perhaps in that black, sleety sky. Then they closed. She began to locomotive again … and then she simply stopped. Whatever had happened was now over. The nurse had seen some of it, the ambulance driver had perhaps seen some of it before he fainted. But it was over now, over for sure. There was only the remains of an ugly accident out here … and a new baby in there.

sahen mich nicht mehr • hinter

Überreste

I looked up at the statue of Harriet White and there she still stood, looking stonily away towards the Garden across the way, as if nothing of any particular note had happened, as if such determination in a world as hard and as senseless as this one meant nothing … or worse still, that it was perhaps the only thing which meant *anything*, the only thing that made any difference at all.

starr • gegenüber • nichts besonders Wichtiges

etwas ausmacht

As I recall, I knelt there in the slush before her severed head and began to weep. As I recall, I was still weeping when an intern and two nurses helped me to my feet and inside.

soweit ich mich erinnere • auf die Beine

McCarron's pipe had gone out.

He relit it with his bolt-lighter while we sat in perfect, breathless silence. Outside, the wind howled and moaned. He snapped his lighter closed and looked up. He seemed mildly surprised to find us still there.

zündete … wieder an • ließ … zuschnappen

'That's all,' he said. 'That's the end! What are you waiting for? Chariots of fire?' He snorted, then seemed to debate for a moment. 'I paid her burial expenses out of my own pocket. She had no one else, you see.' He

Ein Feuerwerk? • schnaubte • zu überlegen • Beerdigungs-

smiled a little. 'Well … there was Ella Davidson, my nurse. She insisted on chipping in twenty-five dollars, which she could ill afford. But when Davidson insisted on a thing –' He shrugged, and then laughed a little.

'You're quite sure it wasn't a reflex?' I heard myself demanding suddenly. 'Are you *quite* sure –'

'Quite sure,' McCarron said imperturbably. 'The first contraction, perhaps. But the completion of her labour was not a matter of seconds but of minutes. And I sometimes think she might have held on even longer, if it had been necessary. Thank God it was not.'

'What about the baby?' Johanssen asked.

McCarron puffed at his pipe. 'Adopted,' he said. 'And you'll understand that, even in those days, adoption records were kept as secret as possible.'

'Yes, but what about the baby?' Johanssen asked again, and McCarron laughed in a cross way.

'You never let go of a thing, do you?' he asked Johanssen.

Johanssen shook his head. 'Some people have learned it to their sorrow. What about the baby?'

'Well, if you've come with me this far perhaps you'll also understand that I had a certain vested interest in knowing how it all came out for that child. Or I felt that I did. There was a young man and his wife – their name was not Harrison, but that is close enough. They lived in Maine. They could have no children of their own. They adopted the child and named him … well, John's good enough, isn't it? John will do you fellows, won't it?'

He puffed at his pipe but it had gone out again. I was faintly aware of Stevens hovering behind me, and knew that somewhere our coats would be at the ready. Soon we would slip back into them … and back into our lives. As McCarron had said, the tales were done for another year.

beizusteuern • sich kaum leisten • zuckte die Achseln
unerschütterlich • Vollendung
durchgehalten
zog an
böse
Kummer
persönlich • was aus dem Kind wurde
ist gut genug für
ich ahnte irgendwie, dass • stand

'The child I delivered that night is now head of the English Department at one of the two or three most respected private colleges in the country,' McCarron said. 'He's not forty-five yet. A young man. It's early for him, but the day may well come when he will be President of that school. I shouldn't doubt it a bit. He is handsome, intelligent, and charming.

'Once, on a pretext, I was able to dine with him in the private faculty club. We were four that evening. I said little and so was able to watch him. He has his mother's determination, gentlemen …

'… and his mother's hazel eyes.'

Leiter

renommiert

charmant • unter einem Vorwand • essen • für den Lehrkörper

Übung 43

Setzen Sie die folgenden Adjektive in den Komparativ und den Superlativ. Aber Vorsicht! Einige sind unregelmäßig.

Adjective	Comparative	Superlative
sure	surer	surest
big		
charming		
good		
respected		
icy		
necessary		

3: The Club

Stevens saw us out as he always did, holding coats, wishing men the happiest of happy Christmases, thanking them for their generosity. I contrived to be the last, and Stevens looked at me with no surprise when I said:

'I have a question I'd like to ask, if you don't mind.'

He smiled a little. 'I suppose you should,' he said. 'Christmas is a fine time for questions.'

Somewhere down the hallway to our left – a hall I had never been down – a grandfather clock ticked sonorously, the sound of the age passing away. I could smell old leather and oiled wood and, much more faintly than either of these the smell of Stevens's aftershave.

'But I should warn you,' Stevens added as the wind rose in a gust outside, 'it's better not to ask too much. Not if you want to keep coming here.'

'People have been closed out for asking too much?' *Closed out* was not really the phrase I wanted, but it was as close as I could come.

'No,' Stevens said, his voice as low and polite as ever. 'They simply choose to stay away.'

I returned his gaze, feeling a chill prickle its way up my back – it was as if a large, cold, invisible hand had been laid on my spine. I found myself remembering that strangely liquid thump I had heard upstairs one night and wondered (as I had more than once before) exactly how many rooms there really *were* here.

'If you still have a question, Mr Adley, perhaps you'd better ask it. The evening's almost over –'

begleitete uns hinaus • Großzügigkeit • es gelang mir

Standuhr • volltönend

schwach • Rasierwasser

wehte böig

ausgeschlossen

nicht mehr zu kommen • hielt • hinaufkriechen • Rücken • dumpf

'And you have a long train-ride ahead of you?' I asked, but Stevens only looked at me impassively. 'All right,' I said. 'There are books in this library that I can't find anywhere else – not in the New York Public Library, not in the catalogues of any of the antiquarian book-dealers I've checked with, and certainly not in *Books in Print*. The billiard table in the Small Room is a Nord. I'd never heard of such a brand, and so I called the International Trademark Commission. They have two Nords – one makes cross-country skis and the other makes wooden kitchen accessories. There's a Seafront jukebox in the Long Room. The ITC has a *Seeburg* listed, but no Sea*front*.'

'What is your question, Mr Adley?'

His voice was as mild as ever, but there was something terrible in his eyes suddenly … no; if I am to be truthful, it was not just in his eyes; the terror I felt had infused the atmosphere all around me. The steady tock-tock from down the lefthand hall was no longer the pendulum of a grandfather clock; it was the tapping foot of the executioner as he watches the condemned led to the scaffold. The smells of oil and leather turned bitter and menacing, and when the wind rose in another wild whoop, I felt momentarily sure that the front door would blow open, revealing not 35th Street but an insane Clark Ashton Smith* landscape where the bitter shapes of twisted trees stood silhouetted on a sterile horizon below which double suns were setting in a gruesome red glare.

Oh, he knew what I had meant to ask; I saw it in his grey eyes.

Where do all these things come from? I had meant to ask. *Oh, I know well enough where* you *come from, Stevens; that accent isn't Dimension X, it's pure Brooklyn. But where do you go? What has put that timeless look in your eyes and stamped it on your face? And, Stevens – where are we RIGHT THIS SECOND?*

ausdruckslos
gefragt
Marke • Markenzeichen • Langlaufskier • Zubehör • eingetragen
erfüllt • auf der linken Seite • Pendel • klopfend • Henker • Verurteilter • Schafott • bedrohlich • Heulen • wahnwitzig • verbogen • sich als Silhouette gegen … abheben • schaurig • Schein
geprägt • in dieser Sekunde

But he was waiting for my question.

I opened my mouth. And the question that came out was: 'Are there many more rooms upstairs?'

'Oh, yes, sir,' he said, his eyes never leaving mine. 'A great many. A man could become lost. In fact, men *have* become lost. Sometimes it seems to me that they go on for miles. Rooms and corridors.'

sich verirren
kein Ende nehmen

'And entrances and exits?'

His eyebrows went up slightly. 'Oh yes. Entrances and exits.'

He waited, but I had asked enough, I thought – I had come to the very edge of something that would, perhaps, drive me mad.

Rand • mich zum Wahnsinn treiben

'Thank you, Stevens.'

'Of course, sir.' He held out my coat and I slipped into it.

'There will be more tales?'

'Here, sir, there are *always* more tales.'

That evening was some time ago, and my memory has not improved between then and now (when a man reaches my age, the opposite is much more likely to be true), but I remember with perfect clarity the stab of

inzwischen • ganz deutlich die plötzliche Angst

info

Clark Ashton Smith (1893–1961) war ein US-amerikanischer Maler, Bildhauer, Dichter und Autor für Fantasy, Horror und Science-Fiction, der hauptsächlich Kurzgeschichten verfasste. Zusammen mit H. P. Lovecraft und Robert E. Howard schrieb er regelmäßig für die Fantasy-Zeitschrift Weird Tales. Er verbrachte fast sein gesamtes Leben mit seinen Eltern in einer kleinen Hütte in Kalifornien. Von 1935 an beschäftigte er sich überwiegend mit der Bildhauerei und dem Malen. Seine Bilder stellen Landschaften und Wesen aus der Fantasy-Welt dar.

fear that went through me when Stevens swung the oaken door wide – the cold certainty that I would see that alien landscape, cracked and hellish in the bloody light of those double suns, which might set and bring on an unspeakable darkness of an hour's duration, or ten hours, or ten thousand years. I cannot explain it, but I tell you that world *exists* – I am as sure of that as Emlyn McCarron was sure that the severed head of Sandra Stansfield went on breathing. I thought for that one timeless second that the door would open and Stevens would thrust me out into that world and I would then hear that door slam shut behind me … forever.

Eichen- • fremdartig • verdorrt • unbeschreiblich • die eine Stunde dauert

endlos • hinausstoßen • zuschlagen

Instead, I saw 35th Street and a radio-cab standing at the curb, exhaling plumes of exhaust. I felt an utter, almost debilitating relief.

das … ausstieß • Auspuffwolken • überwältigend

'Yes, always more tales,' Stevens repeated. 'Goodnight, sir.'

Always more tales.

Indeed there have been. And, one day soon, perhaps I'll tell you another.

Übung 44

Auf welches Wort im Text beziehen sich die folgenden Erklärungen?

1. A sentence which is used to ask for information.
2. To not know where you are.
3. A long, narrow passage between rooms in a building.
4. The curving line of hairs which you have over each eye.
5. A door which leads out of a building or vehicle.
6. To get better.
7. A state in which there is no light.

Lösungen

1

1. conservative – **liberal**
2. question – **answer**
3. damp – **dry**
4. closed – **open**
5. single – **double**
6. tiny – **huge**
7. behind (Präposition) – **in front of**

2

1. [F] Stevens hilft dem Erzähler dabei, seinen Mantel abzulegen.
2. [T] **Laut der Wettervorhersage wird es in der Nacht schneien.**
3. [T] **Stevens fing an, bei dem Klub zu arbeiten, als er eröffnet wurde.**
4. [F] Der Klub hat keinen Namen.
5. [F] Der Klub hat keinen Sekretär.
6. [T] **Der Erzähler arbeitet in einer Anwaltskanzlei.**
7. [F] Der Erzähler ist nicht überrascht, dass er nicht schneller befördert wurde.

3 Waterhouse visits the narrator in his office one day in the **fall**. He leans in the doorway and talks to the narrator about nothing of importance. The narrator expects him to go on to start talking about the cases they are working on, but he doesn't. Instead, he invites the narrator to go with him to a club which he goes to on **Thursday** nights. The narrator is very puzzled by the offer. His wife thinks it means that they are going to **pension** him **off**.

4

1. The narrator **clasps** McCarron's hand briefly.
2. The narrator **felt** a lot out of place.
3. Waterhouse **hasn't deserted** the narrator.
4. Waterhouse **had brought** the narrator a drink.

5

F I X A P K Y O F R
U T E V F O G B E E
K D L O G O T L E B
I R T F K B D I L M
H N A U H T K G I A
A C A P C S B A N Q
U E Y S S E K T G W
R W Q T Q U N O S H
M J O D Q G K R K X
Y L T S O H G Y R J

6

1. [a] The narrator thinks the billiards room door is peculiar because **it is very small**. Der Erzähler findet die Tür zum Billardzimmer seltsam, weil sie sehr klein ist.

2. [a] When the narrator refuses a third martini, Stevens seems **pleased he said no.**
Als der Erzähler einen dritten Martini ablehnt, hat er den Eindruck, dass Stevens sich über seine Ablehnung freut.
3. [c] The chemical powder **causes the flames to change colour.**
Das chemische Pulver bewirkt, dass die Flammen eine andere Farbe bekommen.
4. [b] Gregson doesn't join the others round the hearth because **he wants to practise playing billiards.**
Gregson setzt sich nicht zu den anderen um den Kamin, weil er das Billardspielen üben will.

7
1. The narrator would never have dreamed **of** such a Waterhouse before.
2. Waterhouse's story has to do **with** a teacher who got stuck in a privy.
3. The exhibition is being held **at** the Prudential Center.
4. The teacher was struck dumb **with** embarrassment.
5. The narrator thanks Waterhouse **for** inviting him to the club and sharing the cab.

8
1. S I **M** P L E
2. L A W **Y** E R
3. **S** I D E W A L K
4. **T** H R O A T
5. C H **E** E K
6. C L A **R** I T Y
7. F **I** R M
8. M **O** C K
9. T R **U** T H
10. **S** H O R T

9
unhurriedly (langsam) **slowly**
consumption (Konsum) **intake**
sensation (Gefühl) **feeling**
laughable (lächerlich) **ridiculous**
reflections (Überlegungen) **musings**
precise (genau) **accurate**
story (Geschichte) **tale**
tranquillity (Ruhe) **peace**

10
1. der zwölfte Monat im Jahr: **December** (Dezember)
2. sicher sein, dass etwas wahr ist: **believe** (glauben)
3. ein rauer Wollstoff, aus dem man Jacken macht: **tweed** (Tweed)
4. die Bewegung des großen Organs in der Brust, das Blut durch den Körper pumpt: **heartbeat** (Herzschlag)
5. ein Anlass, zu dem zwei oder mehr Menschen zusammenkommen: **meeting** (Treffen)
6. freudige Erwartung: **excitement** (Aufregung)

11
threat – to threaten – **threatening**
opening – to open – **open**
imagination – to imagine – **imaginative**
dullness – **to dull** – dull

embarrassment – to embarrass – embarrassing
humiliation – to humiliate – humiliating

12
1. [b] I was a little disappointed that I was going to miss Andrews' story.
   Es tat mir leid, dass ich Andrews Geschichte nicht würde hören können.
2. [e] Since then I have read them all and believe them to be eleven of the finest novels of our century.
   Inzwischen habe ich sie alle gelesen und halte sie für elf der schönsten Romane unseres Jahrhunderts.
3. [f] There was some low, goodnatured talk and a burst of laughter.
   Es wurden leise ein paar freundliche Worte gewechselt und ein Lachen klang auf.
4. [a] Cold draughts swirled up the hallway as men slipped out.
   Kalte Luftzüge wirbelten durch die Eingangshalle, als die Herren das Gebäude verließen.
5. [d] I took it into the stacks and found that puzzling, enticing set of green volumes again.
   Ich nahm es mit zu den Bücherregalen und fand die rätselhaften verlockenden grünen Bände wieder.
6. [c] Near the end of the evening there was a story – just one – and Stevens brought brandy around.
   Gegen Ende des Abends wurde eine Geschichte erzählt – nur eine –, und Stevens reichte Brandy dazu.

13
1. The narrator feels as if he is already **a member** of the club.
2. Ellen thinks he's needed something to occupy him **for** a long time.
3. The narrator goes **to sit** beside Ellen on the bed.
4. He can remember **buying** the original hardback edition of the book.
5. There are more **people** than usual at the club on the Thursday before Christmas.
6. The narrator and the other men talk **of** this and that.

14
1. The narrator goes out into the **kitchen** to get some beer.
2. Ellen's book is a brand new **paperback** edition.
3. The narrator bought the original hardback edition for Ellen as a **birthday present**.
4. The narrator finds Stevens's eggnog punch **delicious**.

15
private **sector**
car **accident**
personal **friend**
knife-**fight**
newspaper **photos**
breakfast **table**
coffee **cup**

16
1. Becoming a junior partner means the narrator's salary will rise **by** eight thousand dollars a year.
2. The club members take up a **collection** for Hanrahan's wife.
3. Arlene Hanrahan is a member **of** Ellen's Theatre Society.

17 1. Which of the following words has nothing to do with books?
graduate (Absolvent)
2. Which of the following words does not mean „wahnsinnig“?
goodnatured (freundlich)
3. Which of the following things are not listed in the LMP?
lawyers (Anwälte)
4. Which of the following words has nothing to do with warfare?
sidewalk (Bürgersteig)
5. Which of the following words is not a part of the human body?
awning (Markise)

18 1. ~~foot~~ – brow – chin – cheek
Alle anderen Wörter haben mit dem Kopf zu tun.
2. poem – story – ~~song~~ – tale
Alle anderen Begriffe haben mit Literatur zu tun.
3. taxi – bus – train – ~~bike~~
Alle anderen Wörter beschreiben öffentliche Verkehrsmittel.
4. change – ~~purse~~ – coin – bill
Alle anderen Begriffe beschreiben Geld.
5. huge – enormous – ~~leathery~~ – gigantic
Alle anderen Wörter bedeuten „groß“.
6. Christmas – New Year's Eve – Advent – ~~Thanksgiving~~
Alle anderen Festtage finden im Dezember statt.

19

Y T L E U R C N F E
X V V X U M J V A N
M E D I C A L E S G
K A Q R E Z S Q H I
H L M S E N C T I N
C O Z A E P R T O E
U Q L S Z I S Q N W
N P N V B I O I X O
V O Y P W Z N R H I
N K G G O Y H G L W

20 baby (Baby) – babies
life (Leben) – lives
woman (Frau) – women
lens (Linse) – lenses
business (Unternehmen) – businesses
caveman (Höhlenmensch) – cavemen
closet (Kleiderschrank) – closets
mother-to-be (werdende Mutter) – mothers-to-be
foot (Fuß) – feet
duffer (Dummkopf) – duffers

21

unpleasant	**unangenehm**	glove	**Handschuh**
nowadays	**heutzutage**	sigh	**Seufzer**
responsibility	**Verantwortung**	to hesitate	**zögern**
sleeve	**Ärmel**	condition	**Bedingung**
linen	**Leinen**		

22
1. F Der Arzt sieht der Frau gerade in die Augen.
2. T **Der Arzt wird Mrs Davidson bitten, die Quittungen unter dem Decknamen der Frau auszustellen.**
3. T **Der Arzt meint, dass die Frau mit der Situation sehr gut fertig wird.**
4. F Früher hielt man unverheiratete Frauen, die schwanger wurden, für Huren.
5. T **Die Frau entscheidet sich dafür, dem Arzt ihren richtigen Name zu nennen.**

23
1. Den Mund breiter machen, um zu zeigen, dass man sich freut: **to smile** (lächeln)
2. Ein Kind im Bauch tragend: **pregnant** (schwanger)
3. Ein langer dünner Stab, mit dem man schreibt: **pen** (Stift)
4. Jemand, der von einem Arzt behandelt wird: **patient** (Patient)
5. Kontakte zu Personen, die von Vorteil sind: **connections** (Beziehungen)
6. Sich intensiv mit einem bestimmten Fachgebiet beschäftigen: **to specialize** (sich spezialisieren)
7. Ein ganz kurzer Zeitraum: **instant** (Augenblick)

24 Miss Stansfield hopes that she and the doctor can be friends because this is a frightening time for her. She takes a pad and **pen** from her handbag and asks him about her diet. Dr McCarron gives her a folder with advice on pregnancy which was written by **him**. The doctor is interested in gynaecology but decided not to specialize in it. In his general practice he has still got to deliver over **two** thousand babies.

25
1. **She** puts **it** in **it**.
2. **They** are given **it** by **them**.
3. **He** asks **her** if she wants to keep **it**.

26
1. **poison**
2. **peculiar**
3. **people**
4. **woman**
5. **cash**
6. **receipt**
7. **purse**

Extra-Wort: **appointment**

27
1. A **hospital** is a building where sick people are treated.
2. If you buy something and decide afterwards that you don't want it after all, you can ask for a **refund**.
3. If you have **guts**, then you are a brave person.
4. Another word for human beings in general is **humanity**.
5. To **giggle** means to laugh quickly and quietly.
6. **Advice** is something you give to someone who has a problem and doesn't know what to do.
7. **Garment** is another general word for a piece of clothing.

28

1. A C C O U N T
2. B L I N K
3. T R E M B L E
4. H A Z E L
5. T E A R
6. C O N T R O L
7. S I L E N C E
8. S P E N D
9. N O D

(Lösungswort: UNMARRIED)

29

1. [b] When McCarron doesn't answer the question it seems as if **he might have fallen asleep**.
   Als McCarron die Frage nicht beantwortet, scheint es, als sei er eingedöst.
2. [c] McCarron lights his pipe with a lighter which resembles a **bolt**.
   McCarron zündet seine Pfeife mit einem bolzenartigen Pfeifenanzünder an.
3. [c] **McCarron can't remember** which state Miss Stansfield originally came from.
   McCarron weiß nicht mehr, aus welchem Staat Miss Stansfield ursprünglich kam.
4. [a] Miss Stansfield came to New York to **try to become an actress**.
   Miss Stansfield ist nach New York gekommen, um zu versuchen, Schauspielerin zu werden.

30

1. Many of the women **have been putting** their affairs in order.
2. They **are entering** the valley of the shadow of death.
3. Miss Stansfield **will be having** her baby at the hospital.
4. Dr McCarron **has been giving** her a lot of advice.
5. Miss Stansfield **is looking** forward to the birth of her child.
6. Dr McCarron **has been reading** about the Breathing Method.
7. The mothers-to-be **will** soon **be experiencing** great pain.
8. Many people around the world **have been using** this method for centuries.

31

1. Which of the following words has nothing to do with having a baby?
   cosmetics (Kosmetika)
2. Which of the following words does not apply to Miss Stansfield?
   insane (wahnsinnig)
3. Which of the following does not describe the normal reactions of a patient's relatives to the Breathing Method? **enthusiasm** (Begeisterung)
4. Which of the following cannot be bought at a department store? **cars** (Autos)
5. Which of the following words does not mean „Schmerzen“? **patient** (Patient)

32

1. Miss Stansfield **grew** angry with Mrs Kelly.
2. She kept her eyes fixed **on** Mrs Kelly.
3. He asked **her** what the other use for the Breathing Method was.
4. She was mad as hell **at** Mrs Kelly.
5. Mrs Kelly is always asking if she's **met** a nice boy yet.
6. Miss Stansfield looks at Mrs Kelly **curiously**.

7. Miss Stansfield refuses **to drop** her eyes.
8. She knows what reaction to expect when her secret **comes out**.

33

1. c It wasn't a funny story, perhaps, but I burst out laughing at the image.
   Die Geschichte war vielleicht alles andere als komisch, aber ich brach bei der Vorstellung der Szene in Gelächter aus.
2. g Mrs Kelly yanked open one of her drawers and brought out a buff-coloured cheque.
   Frau Kelly riss eine ihrer Schubladen auf und brachte einen sandfarbenen Scheck zum Vorschein.
3. b I wasn't able to thank her, of course – I was still being a locomotive!
   Bedanken konnte ich mich natürlich nicht – ich war immer noch eine Lokomotive!
4. e The two women looked grimly at each other across a desk littered with perfume samples.
   Über einen Schreibtisch, auf dem Dutzende von Parfümproben herumstanden, starrten sich die beiden Frauen grimmig an.
5. a Mrs Kelly's head rocked back as if she had been slapped.
   Frau Kellys Kopf schnellte zurück, als habe sie eine Ohrfeige erhalten.
6. d I was going to do it; nothing was going to stop me doing it.
   Ich war drauf und dran, es zu tun. Nichts konnte mich davon abhalten.
7. f Mrs Kelly's jaw dropped and her eyes widened.
   Frau Kellys Unterkiefer klappte herunter, und ihre Augen wurden immer größer.

34

F	B	H	H	P	L	L	S	X	H
A	O	F	T	U	R	J	K	P	C
R	O	R	F	A	E	F	A	Z	I
G	R	W	E	J	E	R	E	S	G
U	A	A	F	H	G	R	M	R	A
M	S	O	L	O	E	S	B	Z	M
E	Z	R	T	X	Z	A	L	G	V
N	P	O	N	I	T	T	D	X	B
T	H	S	I	D	E	W	A	L	K
P	L	A	T	S	E	D	E	P	A

35

1. McCarron tells Miss Stansfield that she's not the first **pregnant** woman to feel doomed.
2. This doomed feeling is known amongst doctors as the **Valley** of the Shadow Syndrome.
3. Miss Stansfield is unable to **shake** this feeling.
4. McCarron thinks his joke sounds very **feeble**.
5. McCarron feels the **chill** returning when he tells Miss Stansfield about Harriet White.
6. In his dream Miss Stansfield is carrying **her** head.
7. In his dream Miss Stansfield's linen dress is streaked **with** gore.

36 [1] McCarron wakes up screaming from his nightmare.
McCarron wacht schreiend aus seinem Albtraum auf.
[2] McCarron examines Miss Stansfield on 17 December.
McCarron untersucht Miss Stansfield am 17. Dezember.
[3] Miss Stansfield says she's going to accept the offers of work from the blind woman's friends.
Miss Stansfield sagt, sie werde die Arbeitsangebote von den Freundinnen der blinden Frau annehmen.
[4] Miss Stansfield gives McCarron a Christmas present.
Miss Stansfield gibt McCarron ein Weihnachtsgeschenk.
[5] McCarron sees Miss Stansfield to the door.
McCarron bringt Miss Stansfield zur Tür.
[6] Miss Stansfield stands on tiptoe to kiss McCarron.
Miss Stansfield stellt sich auf die Zehenspitzen, um McCarron zu küssen.
[7] Miss Stansfield says she's sure they'll meet again.
Miss Stansfield sagt, sie sei sicher, dass sie sich wiedersehen werden.

37
1. **sleet**
2. **dangerous**
3. **calm**
4. **accident**
5. **mirror**
6. **spacious**
7. **healthy**

Extra-Wort = **intersection**

38
upside **down**
emergency **wing**
brake-**pedal**
blood-**coloured**
driving **conditions**
final **stage**
cross-**traffic**
severed **head**
black **bag**

39
1. top — **base**
2. front — **rear**
3. beautiful — **hideous**
4. weakness — **strength**
5. upper — **lower**
6. stillness — **movement**
7. stale — **fresh**
8. sane — **mad**
9. to push — **to pull**

40
1. McCarron tells the ambulance attendant to bring him a **blanket**.
2. McCarron strips off his **overcoat**.
3. McCarron opens his black bag and takes out a **scalpel**.
4. When McCarron sees the crown he knows that the baby is **alive**.
5. McCarron is helped by a middle-aged **nurse**.

41
afterwards — **nachher**
naked — **nackt**
unmistakable — **unverkennbar**
steam — **Dampf**
heat — **Wärme**
feebly — **schwach**
mud — **Schlamm**
blanket — **Wolldecke**
perfect — **vollkommen**

42
1. ambulance – ~~socket~~ – stretcher – hospital
   Alle anderen Begriffe haben mit der Gesundheitsfürsorge zu tun.
2. foot – ~~shoe~~ – head – mouth
   Alle anderen Wörter sind Körperteile.
3. ~~statue~~ – lighter – pipe – tobacco
   Alle anderen Begriffe haben mit dem Rauchen zu tun.
4. tongue – lips – teeth – ~~toe~~
   Die anderen Begriffe sind Teile des Mundes.
5. nurse – intern – ~~cabbie~~ – doctor
   Die anderen Menschen arbeiten in einem Krankenhaus.
6. ~~sunshine~~ – sleet – snow – slush
   Alle anderen Begriffe haben mit kaltem Wetter zu tun.

43

Adjective	Comparative	Superlative
sure	surer	surest
big	bigger	biggest
charming	more charming	most charming
good	better	best
respected	more respected	most respected
icy	icier	iciest
necessary	more necessary	most necessary

44
1. Ein Satz, mit dem man um Auskunft bittet: **question** (Frage).
2. Nicht wissen, wo man ist: **to become lost** (sich verirren).
3. Ein langer enger Raum zwischen den Zimmern in einem Gebäude: **corridor** (Gang).
4. Die Bogen aus Haaren, die man über den Augen hat: **eyebrows** (Augenbrauen).
5. Eine Tür, durch die man ein Gebäude oder Fahrzeug verlassen kann: **exit** (Ausgang).
6. Besser werden: **to improve** (sich verbessern).
7. Ein Zustand, in dem es kein Licht gibt: **darkness** (Dunkelheit).

Wörterverzeichnis

A

abbatoir Schlachthof
abdominal Bauch-
abortionist Abtreiber(in)
abroad: to be (was/were – been) abroad draußen sein
abrupt plötzlich
absently zerstreut
to absorb glauben
accepted: to be (was/were – been) quite the accepted thing völlig normal sein
accessories Zubehör
account: before accounts im Voraus
account receivable ausstehend
Accounts Buchhaltung
to accuse vorwerfen
to ache: my hands ache to … ich brenne darauf …
achey head Kopfschmerzen
acting: in acting als Schauspieler(in)
to address anreden
to adjure mahnen
admirable bewundernswert
to admit hereinbitten; einliefern
adrenals Nebennieren
affair Angelegenheit
afterbirth Nachgeburt
aftershave Rasierwasser
afterwards nachher
to age älter werden
agony Qual
to agree: the train didn't agree with me mit dem Zug fuhr ich nicht gern
alchemy Alchemie
alert aufmerksam
alias Deckname
Alice Down the Rabbit-Hole door Tür für Alice im Kaninchenbau (wie in *Alice im Wunderland* von Lewis Carroll)
alien fremdartig
all but fast
amazement: with amazement verblüfft
amber gelb
ambulance attendant Sanitäter(in)
amenity Formalität
amiable: in amiable generalities in liebenswürdigem Ton über allgemeine Dinge
Anglo-Saxon angelsächsisch
animated angeregt
annual jährlich
anonymous anonym
answering service Telefonauftragsdienst
antiquarian book dealer Antiquar(in)
antiquity Antiquität
anxiety Sorge
apparently scheinbar, offensichtlich
appartment-dweller Apartmentbewohner(in)

appearance: to put (put – put) in an appearance sich sehen lassen
application Anwendung
appointment Termin
apprehension Angst
to approve: not to approve of somebody etw. gegen jmd. haben
to approximate ähneln
apt: to be (was/were – been) apt to be something etw. oft werden
apt: to be apt to do something etw. tun können
arch Bogen
aromatic aromatisch
ashamed beschämt
aside from abgesehen von
aspect: from this aspect was das betrifft
ass: Move your ass! Mach schnell!
asshole Arschloch
assiduously fleißig
associated verbunden
to assume membership Mitglied werden
assumed name falscher Name
to assure beruhigen
assured: to be (was/were – been) assured something sich etw. sicher sein
astounded: to be (was/were – been) astounded erstaunt sein
attempt: to make (made – made) no attempt to do something keine Anstalten machen, etw. zu tun
to attend behandeln *Patient*
attendee Besucher(in)
to attest bestätigen
austere herb
avoidance Vermeidung
aware: I was aware of … es war mir bewusst, dass …
awe Ehrfurcht
awkwardness Unsicherheit
awning Markise

B

to babble aloud mit etw. herausplatzen
to back away zurücktreten
backbone Rückgrat
back flap Buchrücken
bag-lady Popsicle gefrorene Stadtstreicherin
bank-book Sparbuch
barber-shop Friseurladen
base Sockel
base of operations Operationsbasis
bastardy Unehelichkeit
to bawl brüllen
to bear (bore – borne): it bears telling man kann es erzählen
to bear ertragen
to bear upon something etw. betreffen
to beat (beat – beaten) hauen
beaver Biberpelz
bed of coals: there was a bed of coals es glühte
bedrock Grundstock
bedrock-practical unsentimental und praktisch
to befriend helfen
to believe something to be etw. halten für
bellow Schrei
bellowing stürmisch
belly Bauch(muskeln)
bemusement Verwirrung
benevolence Feuerstelle

benign gutartig
bereavement schmerzlicher Verlust
better than mehr als
between then and now inzwischen
bewildered verwirrt
beyond hinter
to bid (bade – bidden) someone goodbye sich von jmdm. verabschieden
bill Schein
birth: giving birth Entbinden
to birth: those who birthed us diejenigen, die unsere Vorfahren waren
birth cycle Geburtszyklus
bitch Schlampe
to bite (bit – bitten) off nicht sagen
blade Klinge
bladelike scharf
bland fade
blanket Wolldecke
blast: at full blast auf vollen Touren
bleeding-heart weichlich
to bless segnen
blood-drenched blutgetränkt
blood-grimed blutverschmiert
blood-loss: to die of blood-loss verbluten
blooming blühend
blotch Fleck
to blow (blew – blown) pusten
blown im Wind tanzend
blown off: to be (was/were – been) blown off abgerissen werden
boarding house Pension
boil Furunkel
bold as brass frech wie Oskar
boltlike bolzenartig
bone white schlohweiß
to bother to do something sich die Mühe machen, etw. zu tun
bowel cramps Darmkrämpfe
bowling alley Kegelbahn
brand Marke
brawny kräftig
to break (broke – broken) down sein Schweigen brechen
breathing method Atemtechnik
breathlessly atemlos
brick Ziegelstein
bricky ziegelrot
brief Schriftsatz
brief(ly) kurz
bright sonnig
brilliantly strahlend
to brim in Tränen schwimmen
brittle spröde
broad Tussi
broad-mindedness Toleranz
broadside um die eigene Achse
to broil braten
broken unterbrochen
brow Stirn
brownstone Haus mit rötlich-braunem Sandstein
buff-coloured sandfarben
to bulge: his eyes were bulging from their sockets ihm fielen fast die Augen aus dem Kopf
bulging hervorgetreten
bump Aufschlag
to bump and ridge over something sich über etw. unregelmäßig ausbreiten
burial Beerdigung
to burst (burst – burst) out hervorstoßen
to burst out laughing in Gelächter ausbrechen

bushy buschig
business: to have (had – had) no business doing something kein Recht haben, etw. zu tun
business: to mean (meant – meant) business es ernst meinen
business: in the plumbing or carpentry business als Klempner oder Tischler
businesslike sachlich, geschäftsmäßig
butcher abortionist Engelmacher(in)
to button zuknöpfen
to buzz somebody jmd. rufen
buzzard Geier, gierige Person
buzzy: my head was a trifle buzzy es summte ein bisschen in meinem Kopf

C

cabbie Taxifahrer(in)
caboose Hinterteil
cadaverous ausgezehrt
caked verkrustet
call: to be (was/were – been) on call in Bereitschaft sein
to cancel absagen
candlestick-maker Kerzenmacher(in)
capful Verschlusskappe
carrying deutlich
cartwheel rund
case: in no case aber nein
case citation Fallzitat
cash: on a cash basis bar
cashier's check Bankscheck
to cast (cast – cast) werfen
castle keep Festungsturm
casualties Tote und Verwundete
to catch (caught – caught) stocken
caveman Höhlenmensch
centrepuncher jmd., der die Vorarbeit leistet
ceremony: to stand (stood – stood) on ceremony Wert auf Förmlichkeiten legen
cervix Muttermund
chagrined: to feel (felt – felt) chagrined sich ärgern
to chance riskieren
channel Dienstweg
change Kleingeld
charge: on charges of wegen
chariots of fire Feuerwerk (wörtlich: Streitwagen aus Feuer)
charley horse Muskelkater
charming charmant
to chart messen
to chase verfolgen
check: to be (was/were – been) in check auf dem Spiel stehen
to check out durchsuchen
to check over untersuchen
to check through durchsuchen
to check with fragen
Checker *Art amerikanisches Taxi*
checkered kariert
checkup Untersuchung
cheer: good cheer Bereitwilligkeit
chestnut Ratschlag
chill Schauder
chillingly schrecklich
to chip in beisteuern
chippie Schlampe
to chisel einmeißeln
Christian name Vorname
cinders Asche
circumstances (unglückliche) Umstände

to clap to halten an
to clap one's hands together in die Hände klatschen
clapper Klöppel
clarity: with perfect clarity ganz deutlich
to clasp drücken; verschränken
class gesellschaftliche Stellung
to clear sich verziehen
to clear one's throat sich räuspern
to clench zusammenbeißen; sich zusammenziehen
click Klicken
to climb by sich erhöhen um
clink Klirren
cloche hat Kapotthut
clogged verstopft
to close on sich nähern
to close out ausschließen
closed circuit TV camera Überwachungskamera
closely prüfend
closet Kleiderschrank
to clutch one's hands die Hände verschränken
to coincide zusammenfallen
cold front Kaltluftfront
coldly betont kühl
collection Sammlung
colourless nichtssagend
to come (came – come) by finden
to come out: how it all came out for that child was aus dem Kind wurde
to come out bekannt werden
to come to be gegründet werden
comfortable umgänglich; gut
comfortably off wohlhabend
Commission on Women's Rights Frauenrechtskommission
common gewöhnlich
to communicate with führen zu
community theatre Laienspielgruppe
complacent selbstzufrieden
complete vollkommen
complete: the complete so-and-so die gesammelten Werke von Soundso
completion Vollendung
composed beherrscht
composure Selbstbeherrschung
conception Empfängnis; Vorstellung
concern: she did it out of concern for … sie hat es getan, weil sie um … besorgt war
to concern oneself with sich befassen mit
to concoct zaubern
concussion Aufprall
the condemned die Verurteilten
condition Bedingung; Verfassung
congress: we had little more congress wir hatten uns kaum gesehen
to consider betrachten
considerate diskret
consignment Wagenladung
consulting room Sprechzimmer
to contemplate planen
contemptuous verächtlich
contractions Wehen
contractive labour Eröffnungsperiode
contrary: to the contrary dagegen
to contribute beitragen
to contrive: I contrived to … es gelang mir …
convergence Annäherung

conversational gesprochen
to convert umtauschen
convinced überzeugt
to cope with something mit etw. zurechtkommen
copyright Copyright
to corkscrew up hinaufstieben
corpse Leiche
cost-efficient kostengünstig
costume jewellery Modeschmuck
count: at last count nach der letzten Zählung
to counterbalance ausgleichen
counterpane Bettdecke
course: over a course of weeks wochenlang
covers Bettdecke
to crack something a blow sich etw. stoßen
cracked verdorrt
to crash to the floor krachend zu Boden fallen
to crawl up sich überziehen
crazed verrückt
credit: to her credit es macht ihr große Ehre
to creep (crept – crept) away sich davonschleichen
crêpe-soled Kreppsohlen-
to crop up auftauchen
cross: in a cross way böse
to cross: the thought crossed my mind der Gedanke war mir schon gekommen
crossbones gekreuzte Knochen
cross-country ski Langlaufski
crossed: to be (was/were – been) crossed by scheitern an
cross-traffic vorbeifahrende Fahrzeuge
crown Kopf
to crown: the baby crowned der Kopf des Babys wurde sichtbar
crucially besonders
crude grob
to cruise langsam fahren
crumpled zerknittert
to cry out schreien
crystal (ball) Kristallkugel
cue Einsatzzeichen
cum mit
to cup halten
to curdle gerinnen
curse Fluch
cursed unglücklich
cursory flüchtig
curtain: to draw (drew – drawn) a curtain over something etw. lassen
curtly schroff
to cut (cut – cut) streichen
cuttingly gnadenlos
to cycle from wechseln von
cyclone shape Zyklonform
cynic Zyniker(in)

D

to dance funkeln
to dangle herunterbaumeln
darkish dunkel
dazed benommen, betäubt
dead: to stop dead wie angewurzelt stehen bleiben
death: to frighten someone to death jmd. zu Tode erschrecken
death-warrant Todesurteil
to debate sich überlegen
debilitating überwältigend
decapitated geköpft
to deceive betrügen

decent: to do (did – done) the decent thing tun, was sich gehört
decorum Grazie, Sitten
to deepen sich steigern
to define bestimmen
delicate verwundbar
delicate: in a delicate condition in anderen Umständen
to deliver entbinden
to deliver a child ein Kind zur Welt bringen
to deliver someone jmd. entbinden
delivery room Kreißsaal
deluded: to be (was/were – been) deluded sich Illusionen machen
deposit Kaution
depressing bedrückend
to desert im Stich lassen
destruction Sachbeschädigung
to deter somebody from doing something jmd. davon abhalten, etw. zu tun
determined willensstark
diet Ernährung
difference: to make (made – made) a difference etw. ausmachen
dignified respektvoll
dignity Würde
dilated geöffnet
dim dunkel
dime-store billig
to dine essen
dine or sumpin (dying or something) starb oder so etwas
dinner: to have (had – had) someone to dinner jmd. zum Abendessen einladen
dinner jacket Smokingjacke
direct gerade
direct hit Volltreffer
directive Weisung
dirty scheußlich
disgust Entrüstung, Abscheu
dismembered zertrümmert
dismemberment Zerstückelung
disorientation Desorientierung
distinct einzeln
distressed betrübt
divorced getrennt
to do (did – done): that will do you das ist gut genug für Sie
docile fügsam
Dodgem Car Autoskooter
dog: to die a dog's death elend zugrunde gehen
dome-light Leuchtbuchstaben
donkey's years ago vor langer Zeit
doomed (zum Untergang) verdammt
door: to show someone the door jmdm. die Tür weisen
doorman Portier
dotage: to be (was/were – been) in one's dotage langsam senil werden
double doorway Doppeltür
doze Nickerchen
doze: to fall (fell – fallen) into a doze eindösen
to drain from weichen aus
drama critic Theaterkritiker(in)
dramatics: to do (did – done) high school dramatics in der Schule Theater spielen
draught Luftzug
draughty zugig
to draw (drew – drawn) ziehen an
to draw away losfahren
to draw up heranziehen; anhalten

drawn: to be (was/were – been) drawn to angezogen sein von
dreamy abwesend
dress Kleidung
drift: to catch (caught – caught) someone's drift jmd. verstehen
to drift away from someone jmdm. nicht mehr zuhören
drifting treibend
to drink (drank – drunk) to something auf etw. trinken
to drive (drove – driven) treiben
driving conditions Straßenverhältnisse
to drop sinken; herunterklappen
to drop by hereinschauen bei, vorbeikommen
to drop in vorbeikommen
to drown ertrinken
to drown out übertönen
druggist Apotheker(in)
due: to be (was/were – been) due somebody jmdm. zustehen
due date errechnetes Geburtsdatum
dues Mitgliedsbeitrag
duffer: old duffer alter Dummkopf
to dull lindern
dumb: to be (was/were – been) struck dumb with something von etw. wie gelähmt sein
duration: of an hour's duration die eine Stunde dauert

E

eagerly mit Eifer
easy leicht zu haben
eave Dachgesims
ebony Ebenholz
edge Rand; Rand der Mittellosigkeit
edge: to take (took – taken) the edge off something etw. abschwächen
to edge: to be (was/were – been) edging past one kurz nach eins sein
edging Ränder
eerily gespenstisch
effect: the one to the effect that … nämlich, dass …
eggnog punch Eierpunsch
eight to the bar aber im Takt
embarrassment Verlegenheit
to embrace annehmen
emergency Notfall
emergency basis Notlage
employ: to be (was/were – been) in somebody's employ bei jmdm. beschäftigt sein
endtable kleiner Tisch
to endure beständig sein
engaged: to engage in the usual behaviour sich gewöhnlich verhalten
enquiring fragend
to enroll in sich anmelden zu
to enter beginnen; erreichen
enterprise Unternehmen
to entertain haben
enticing verlockend
epistle Epistel
errand Besorgung
ether Äther
eve Abend
examination table Untersuchungstisch
to examine untersuchen
exasperation Verzweiflung
to exchange austauschen
excruciatingly painful qualvoll

executioner Henker
exhale Exhalation, Ausatmen
to exhale ausstoßen
exhaust Auspuff
to exhibit zeigen
expectant werdend
to expel herauspressen
expense(s) Kosten
expulsion Ausscheidung
eye: ... caught my eye mein Blick fiel auf ...
eye: to have (had – had) one's eye on something ein Auge auf etw. geworfen haben
eye: to lay eyes on somebody jmd. zu Gesicht bekommen
eyeball Augapfel

F

to face ins Auge sehen
fact: as a matter of fact ehrlich gesagt
faculty Lehrkörper
to fade verblassen
failure Fehlschlag
to faint dead away bewusstlos in sich zusammensinken
faintly schwach; dunkel
fair: that's fair enough das kann ich verstehen
fairness: in all fairness gerechterweise
fall Herbst
to fall (fell – fallen) into conversation with somebody mit jmdm. ins Gespräch kommen
to fall into a discussion of something anfangen, etw. zu diskutieren
far from it weit gefehlt
fare Fahrgast
fashion Manier
to favour beehren
fearful ungeheuer
feature Gesichtsausdruck
feeble lahm
feebly schwach
feeling: to hurt (hurt – hurt) somebody's feelings jmd. kränken
feet: to be (was/were – been) back on one's feet wieder auf den Beinen sein
feet: he helped me to my feet er half mir auf die Beine
fellow creature Mitmensch
fender-bender Bagatellunfall
feverish: to a feverish pitch fieberhaft
fiction: work of fiction Roman
fiend Teufel
to figure eine Rolle spielen
filthy gemein
final kick Endspurt
fine gut
finger-wave Ringellöckchen
fireplace Kamin, Feuerstelle
firm fest
first: from the first von Anfang an
to fishtail schleudern
to fix on sich richten auf
to flag heranwinken
flair Talent
flanking operation Flankenoperation
to flash blinken
flasher Licht
flatbed truck Tieflader
flattery Schmeichelei
to flip werfen
flow of humanity Menschenstrom

flurry Schneeschauer
to flurry: it had been flurrying es hatte Schneeschauer gegeben
flush Erröten
to flutter zittern, aufgeregt sein
fluttery verstimmt *Magen*
focus: her eyes lost their focus ihre Augen sahen mich nicht mehr
to focus one's attention on sich konzentrieren auf
to foist something on somebody jmdm. etw. andrehen
folder Faltblatt, Akte
folderol Firlefanz
folio volume Folioband
fontanell Fontanelle
fool: to be (was/were – been) fool enough to do something dumm genug sein, um etw. zu tun
footman Diener
forbidding unnahbar
force Gewalt, Wucht
forceps Zange
forearm Unterarm
to forecast (forecast – forecast) voraussagen
to foresee (foresaw – foreseen) vorhersehen
form: for the sake of form um die Form zu wahren
formidable beeindruckend
formless formlos
forth: to bring (brought – brought) forth zur Welt bringen
forwarding address Nachsendeadresse
foul schlecht
frankly offen
freakishly seltsamerweise
free-verse aus freien Versen
frenziedly wild
frightful grässlich
frigid eisig
frost crystal Eiskristall
frost-rimmed von Eisblumen bedeckt
to frown die Stirn runzeln
frustrated frustriert
full-day pass Tageskarte
full-time member Vollmitglied
to fumble one's way into silence die richtigen Worten nicht finden und schweigen
to fumble with herumfingern an
fumigator Kammerjäger
fuzzy undeutlich

G

gadget Instrument
gaily wrapped hübsch verpackt
gainful employment Erwerbstätigkeit
gall Galle
gas Gaspedal
gaunt hager
generalities allgemeine Dinge
generosity Großzügigkeit
to get (got – got/gotten) down to something sich zu etw. wenden
ghostly geisterhaft, gespenstisch
giddy leichtsinnig
gilt vergoldet
gingery rötlich
girdle Korsett
glare Schein
glassy intensiv
glaze of ice Glatteis
glibly leichtfertig
to glimpse flüchtig sehen
glove Handschuh

gnarled knotig
to go (went – gone) on to nachher gehen zu
to go out from under one unter einem wegrutschen
to go up dehnen, sich erstrecken
God-awful ekelig
god damned gottverdammt
going: when the going gets tough wenn es hart auf hart kommt
good: for good für immer
goodnatured freundlich
goodnaturedly freundschaftlich
gooseflesh Gänsehaut
gown Gewand
grace Anstand
grace: with good grace mit Fassung
graduate Absolvent(in)
grammar school teacher Gymnasiallehrer(in)
grandfather clock Standuhr
to grant: I grant you that das gebe ich zu
to grasp begreifen
grating Gitter
to graze weiden
grimly grimmig
to grope for fingern nach, tasten nach
to growl knurren
grudging spirit Widerwillen
gruesome grausig, schaurig
grunting ächzend
guest book Gästebuch
to guide leiten
gust: to rise (rose – risen) in a gust böig wehen
guts Eingeweide
guts: to have (had – had) guts Schneid haben
gutter Gosse
gutter-word Kraftausdruck
gymnasium Fitnessraum
gynaecology Gynäkologie

H

hack Droschke
had: to be (was/were – been) had zu finden sein
half: half-walk, half-run teils gehen, teils laufen
half: not half bad gar nicht schlecht
half: too smart by half schon frech genug
half-unbuttoned halb aufgeknöpft
hand: to change hands den Besitzer wechseln
hand: at hand vorliegend
hand: to raise one's hands in horror entsetzt sein
to handle behandeln
hangman Henker
happenstance Zufall
hardback gebunden
hardening Anspannung
to hatch aushecken
hazel haselnussbraun
head Leiter(in)
head: to bring (brought – brought) to a head zum Überschäumen bringen
to head leiten
healthful gesund
heaping gehäuft
heard: yet to be heard from noch unbekannt
hearth Kamin
heat Wärme
heathenish heidnisch
to heave sich heben

heel of one's palm Handballen
to heighten sich verstärken
to help: to be (was/were – been) unable to help it nichts dafür können
hem Saum
here: here you go bitte schön
to hesitate zögern
hideous grässlich
high: the colour was high in her cheeks ihre Wangen waren rot
high-ceilinged mit hoher Decke
hilarious urkomisch
to hire einstellen
to hitch wiederkommen
to hold (held – held) on durchhalten
to hold up sich halten
hole Lücke
homesickness Heimweh
homily Spruch
honorarium Honorar
to hover stehen; liegen
howling heulend
Howwuzzit? (How was it?) Wie war's?
Huh? Nicht wahr?
hum Summen
humiliation Demütigung
to hyperventilate hyperventilieren
hyperventilation Hyperventilation
to hypnotize hypnotisieren
hypocrisy Heuchelei
hysteria Hysterie

I

idea Ahnung
identical eineiig
to idle leerlaufen
if that wenn überhaupt
ill afford: to be (was/were – been) able to ill afford something sich etw. kaum leisten können
imaginative fantasievoll
immune: to be (was/were – been) immune to immun sein gegen
impassively ausdruckslos
impending drohend
imperturbably unerschütterlich
impish(ly) spitzbübisch
imprint Impressum
in: there will be something in it es springt etw. dabei heraus
to inch kriechen
incident Vorfall
income jump sprunghafter Einkommensanstieg
to incriminate belastend ausfallen für
indefinable undefinierbar
to index in den Index aufnehmen
indifferent gleichgültig
inept ungeschickt
inexcusable unverzeihlich
infant Baby
infernal teuflisch
infinity: to infinity ohne Ende
to inflict somebody with something jmdm. etw. zufügen
infused erfüllt
inhale Inhalation
initial erst
inlaid board Brett mit Einlegearbeit
insane wahnsinnig, wahnwitzig
inscription Inschrift
to inspire inspirieren
instance Anfall
instruction Weisung
insupportable unerträglich
intake of alcohol Alkoholkonsum

interest: to express an interest in doing something sein Interesse bekunden, etw. zu tun
intern Assistenzarzt, -ärztin
to intern Assistenzarzt sein
internship Praktikum
interrogative fragend
interruption Unterbrechung
interval Abstand
intestines Eingeweide
to investigate lüften
to issue ausstellen
ivory Elfenbein

J

jagged abgebrochen
jammed: to get (got – got/gotten) something jammed in something mit etw. in etw. stecken bleiben
janitor Hausmeister(in)
JayCee Junior
jerky zuckend
to jet schießen
to join beitreten; sich gesellen zu
to join someone mitlachen
jolting rumpelnd
to jot aufschreiben
to jump zusammenfahren
just: it's just as well das ist gut so
to jutt out hervorragen

K

keen scharf
keenly sehr
to keep (kept – kept) verbringen; bewahren; haben
to keep somebody from doing something jmd. davor bewahren, etw. zu tun
to keep up with something mit etw. auf dem Laufenden bleiben
kerb Bordstein
keystone Mittelstein
kindliness Güte
knife-fight Messerstecherei
knot Knorren
knowingly absichtlich

L

labour Arbeit; Geburt
ladylike damenhaft
to lance aufstechen
latched verriegelt
late: to stay late Überstunden machen
to laugh out loud laut auflachen
to leap (leapt – leapt) schießen
leathery ledern
lefthand auf der linken Seite
legitimate traditionell
length: to run (ran – run) the length of something sich über die ganze Länge von etw. erstrecken
lens Linse
lest damit nicht
to let (let – let) down im Stich lassen
to let oneself out sich die Tür aufmachen
to let up nachlassen
level Pegel
level: on the level of genauso wie
librarian Bibliothekar(in)
licentiousness Unzüchtigkeit
lie: to tell (told – told) somebody a lie jmd. belügen
life-cycle Lebenszyklus
life-force Lebenskraft

light Erleuchtung
light: in light of this bei diesem Stand der Dinge
to light (lit – lit) anzünden
liquid dumpf
linen Leinen
link Glied
lip: to rise (rose – risen) to one's lips auf der Zunge liegen
to list eintragen
listing: I found no listing for … … war nicht aufgeführt
litter Wurf
littered: the desk was littered with … auf dem Schreibtisch standen … herum
to live on something von etw. leben
livery: in livery livriert
load Last
loading door Hintertür
to loan leihen
loathing Abscheu
locale Ort
to lock together ineinander verkrallen
locked stramm
lodgings möbliertes Zimmer
log Scheit
long: that was the long and the short of it das war alles
to look at beurteilen
to loom up sich abzeichnen
lost: to become (became – become) lost sich verirren
low leise
to luck onto something etw. zufällig finden
ludicrous lächerlich
lumberjack shirt Holzfällerhemd
lunatic Verrückte(r)
lustrously hell
lying betrügerisch

M

mad: to drive (drove – driven) mad zum Wahnsinn treiben
mad as hell furchtbar wütend
maddening verrückt machend
madhouse Irrenanstalt
magnifying vergrößernd
mahogany-panelled mahagonigetäfelt
maiden unverheiratet
to make (made – made) up one's mind on the subject sich dazu entschließen
malfeasance Vergehen
malignant bösartig
mamma rat Rattenweibchen
mantle Ummantelung
marble Murmel
margin Rand
to mark bemerken
to match somebody stride for stride mit jmdm. Schritt halten
matchwood Kleinholz
to materialize auftauchen
matted with blood blutgetränkt
measured gleichmäßig
medical: in medical procedure in der Medizin
medicine: to practise medicine den Arztberuf ausüben
medico Sanitäter(in)
mellowly matt
membrane Membran
menacing bedrohlich
mental geistig

mention: to make (made – made) no mention of something etw. nicht erwähnen
messjacket Messjackett
metaphor: in metaphor im übertragenen Sinne
mid-labour Austreibungsperiode
mid-level mittlere
midpoint: at the midpoint of mitten in
mid-shin: at about mid-shin kurz über dem Fußgelenk
midwest im Mittleren Westen
mile: to go (went – gone) on for miles kein Ende nehmen
milquetoast zaghaft
mind Kopf, Verstand
mind: in my mind's eye im Geiste
miscarriage Fehlgeburt
mistaken: to be (was/were – been) mistaken sich täuschen
mixed unterschiedlich
to mock spotten
modulations of sound unartikulierte Laute
morgue Leichenschauhaus
morphine Morphium
mother-to-be werdende Mutter
moue Blick
to mount anbringen; hinaufsteigen
to mouth formen
mud Schlamm
mule for work Arbeitspferd
to mull something over sich etw. durch den Kopf gehen lassen
murk dämmrige Tiefe, Finsternis
musing Überlegung
muted gedämpft
mutilated verstümmelt
muzzy unklar

N

naked nackt
to name benennen
new-minted brandneu
newsstand Kiosk
next to nothing kaum etw.
nigger Neger
nitrous oxide Lachgas
noose Schlinge
to nose one's way out of langsam verlassen
notable bemerkenswert
note: nothing of any note nichts Wichtiges
notice: at short notice kurzfristig
nowadays heutzutage
nuisance Übel
numb betäubt
nursing Krankenpflege

O

oaken Eichen-
obligatory obligatorisch
obscure obskur
obstetrics Geburtshilfe
occasion: on another occasion ein anderes Mal
ocelot Ozelot
odd: at odd moments ab und zu
oink grunz
to oink grunzen
oinker Grunzer
one-of-a-kind-ness Einzigartigkeit
onset Anfang
opinion: to hold (held – held) an opinion sich ein Urteil erlauben
opposite: to play opposite die Gegenrolle spielen zu
optic nerve Sehnerv

orbit Höhle
out-of-date altmodisch
out of place fehl am Platz
outpatient referral Patient, der von der Poliklinik überwiesen worden ist
overdue: I am overdue on my next patient mein nächster Patient wartet schon auf seinen Termin
overly besonders
to overspill überlaufen
to overstep zu weit gehen
overweight übergewichtig
own: on her own alleinstehend
oxygen Sauerstoff

P

to pace langsam vorankommen
to pack oneself into something sich in etw. zwängen
pad Notizblock
palate: to have (had – had) a palate einen feinen Gaumen haben
pamphlet Merkblatt
to pant keuchen, hecheln
pants Hose
paralyzing sehr heftig
parquet floor Parkettfußboden
parted geöffnet
to participate in teilnehmen an
parti-coloured teilweise farbig
to pass out ohnmächtig werden; austeilen
passed off vorbei
passing lane Überholspur
passionate leidenschaftlich
to patter prasseln
pavilion Pavillon
pawnshop Pfandhaus
peach of a day herrlicher Tag
peculiar seltsam
pedestal Podest
pelvic-area Becken-
pendulum Pendel
to pension off pensionieren
perception Wahrnehmung
perfect vollkommen
permission Erlaubnis
to persist nicht lockerlassen
pestle-pounder Pillendreher(in)
phone: to get (got – got/gotten) someone on the phone jmd. am Apparat haben
phrasing Formulierung
physician Arzt, Ärztin
pick-up Abholen
picnic hamper Picknickkorb
to picture something in one's mind sich etw. vorstellen
pier glass *Art großer Spiegel*
pilot-light Zündflamme
pinball bowling game Flipperspiel
pipe-lighter Pfeifenanzünder
pique Ärger
placenta Plazenta
plastered to the hairline blau wie ein Veilchen
platter Platte
pleasantry Höflichkeit
please: if you please wenn es Ihnen recht ist
plume Strom, Wolke
to plunge ahead fortfahren
point: I take your point ich verstehe
point: at one point einmal
to point towards … in Richtung auf … gehen
pointer Zeigestock
to poise *(Stift)* in Schreibposition nehmen

poison ivy Efeuvergiftung
policy: it is not my policy to … ich mache es mir nicht zum Grundsatz zu …
to ponder nachsinnen über
pool of light Lichtinsel
Popsicle Eis am Stiel
positive sicher
to pound stampfen
power: to run (ran – run) at full power auf vollen Touren sein
practice Praxis
precognitive interlude Vorahnung
to predict erwarten
pregnancy: to be (was/were – been) two months gone in pregnancy seit zwei Monaten schwanger sein
preliminary Vor-
pre-natal pränatal
preoccupied beschäftigt
prep(aration) Vorbereitung
prescient weitblickend
to press somebody into service to do something jmd. bitten, etw. zu tun
pretext: on a pretext unter einem Vorwand
pretty: as pretty as the day so schön wie der Frühling selbst
to prickle its way up hinaufkriechen
private-sector auf dem privaten Sektor
privy Klosett
professional ethics Berufsethik
to progress fortschreiten
promptly pünktlich
pronouncement Feststellung
proper korrekt
properly speaking eigentlich
to prove the point etw. beweisen
publication: to be (was/were – been) an annual publication jährlich erscheinen
to puff schnaufen
to puff at ziehen an
to puke kotzen
to pull up halten
pulse-rate Pulsfrequenz
to punch through durchstechen durch
punctilious förmlich
punctured perforiert
to purport to be something angeblich etw. sein sollen
put out: to be (was/were – been) put out with someone auf jmd. böse sein
puzzling rätselhaft

Q

qualm: with never a qualm ohne das geringste Bedauern
quarter Vierteldollar
queer seltsam
quilt Steppdecke

R

rack Stange
radiant strahlend
to radiate ausstrahlen
radio cab Funktaxi
rag-doll Stoffpuppe
railing Geländer
rampway Rampe
rather eher
rationale Begründung
to reacquaint oneself with something neue Freundschaft mit etw. schließen

to read (read – read) aloud vorlesen
readily bereitwillig
rear view mirror Rückspiegel
to rebound abprallen
to recall sich erinnern an
to recall something to somebody's mind jmd. an etw. erinnern
to recant bereuen
receipt Quittung
recessed zurückgesetzt
record Aufzeichnung
to recount erzählen
rectitude Korrektheit
recurrence Wiederkehr
to reduce somebody to something jmd. zu etw. machen
reed Rohrblatt
to refer überweisen
reference room Raum für Nachschlagewerke
reflection Spiegelbild
refund: to issue a refund eine Rückvergütung vornehmen
to register at sich anmelden in
to reiterate wiederholen
Relief Committee Sozialhilfeausschuss
to relight wiederanzünden
reluctantly widerstrebend
remains Überreste
remorselessly unerbittlich
to render machen
rent-balance Mietdifferenz
to repay vergelten
to request verlangen
required: to be (was/were – been) required to do something etw. tun müssen
reserve Zurückhaltung
respectable ordentlich
respected renommiert
responsibility Verantwortung
rest: to come (came – come) to rest zum Stillstand kommen
to resume wiederanfangen
retarded geistig behindert
to return halten
to rev up auf Touren kommen
review Kritik
rid: to be (was/were – been) rid of loswerden
ride Attraktion
ridge: the ridge of his brow seine Stirn
ridiculous lächerlich
right this second in dieser Sekunde
to rinse färben
to rise (rose – risen) aufstehen; aufsteigen
to rise above aufsteigen über
roar Brüllen
to roar brüllen
roaring lodernd
robe Bademantel
to rock back zurückschnellen
round-heels lose
rubber stamp Stempel
ruefully traurig
rule: as a rule normalerweise
rumble Rumpeln
run Strecke
ruptured zerfetzt
to rustle rascheln

S

salubrious bekömmlich
salutary günstig
to salute bewundern
salvation Erlösung
sample Probe

to sand Sand streuen
sap Saft
sarge Sergeant
sawbones Medizinmann
scaffold Schafott
scalpel Skalpell
schedule Plan
scheduled: to be (was/were – been) scheduled to be taken away abtransportiert werden sollen
to scoff spotten
scrape Schaber
scrape: to get (got – got/gotten) into a scrape in Schwulitäten kommen
to scribble kritzeln
to scutter flitzen
security Sicherheit
to seduce verführen
to see (saw – seen) out hinausbegleiten
seed envelope Samentüte
to seep durchsickern
to seize packen; überkommen
to seize on aufgreifen
semi-circle Halbkreis
sense: to lose (lost – lost) one's senses den Verstand verlieren
to sense as halten für
senseless sinnlos
seriously schwer
seriousness Ernst
set Gesamtausgabe *Bücher*; Haltung
to settle into something es sich in etw. bequem machen
to settle on fallen auf
severance pay Abfindungsgeld
severance slip Abfindungsbestätigung
severed abgetrennt, abgerissen
sex Geschlecht
shade Ton
shadow of death Todesschatten
to shake (shook – shaken) abschütteln
shallow flach
sheet-welder Schweißer(in)
shell Granate
shellshocked von der Detonation betäubt
to shelve ins Regal stellen
to shift wechseln
shilly-shallying unentschlossen
shingle: to hang (hung – hung) out one's shingle sich selbstständig machen
shore Küste
shortly bald
shoulderblade Schulterblatt
to show: I am showing es fällt auf, dass ich schwanger bin
to shriek kreischen
shrivelled geschrumpft
shroud Schleier
shudder Schauder
shudder: a shudder worked up my spine es lief mir kalt den Rücken hinunter
sidewalk Bürgersteig
sigh Seufzer
silage Silofutter
silhouetted: to stand (stood – stood) silhouetted on sich als Silhouette abheben gegen
sink or swim: to leave (left – left) somebody to sink or swim jmd. im Stich lassen
to sip at nippen an
skill Fertigkeit

to skitter rutschen
skull Totenkopf
slam Zuschlagen
to slam knallen
to slam shut zuschlagen
to slap: to be (was/were – been) slapped eine Ohrfeige erhalten
to slap something into somebody's hand jmdm. etw. in die Hand drücken
sleet Schneeregen
sleety graupelig
sleeve Ärmel
slender schlank
slick schlüpfrig
to slide (slid – slid) schieben; schleudern
to slide open aufziehen
slight schmächtig
to slip ausrutschen
to slip away sich davonmachen; verloren gehen, verfliegen
slithery dumpf
slogger Arbeitstier
slope-shouldered mit abfallenden Schultern
sloppily rührselig
slush Schneematsch
smart schick; frech
to smart schmerzen
smartly gewissenhaft
to smash into prallen gegen
smooth mild
to smooth out sich entspannen
to snap at anfahren
to snap closed/shut zuschnappen lassen
snarled chaotisch
to snatch away verschlingen
to sniff die Nase rümpfen
snifter Schwenker
snobbery Snobismus
to snort schnauben
so-and-so Soundso
to sober ernst werden
socially: to see (saw – seen) somebody socially sich mit jmdm. privat treffen
socket Höhle
soda Limo
solicitude Zuwendung
sonourously volltönend
sorrow Kummer
soundless lautlos
spark Funke
specific Einzelheit
speckled gesprenkelt
to speed (sped – sped) up schneller werden
speedily schnell
to spike down befestigen
to spin (spun – spun) out erzählen
spinal block Rückenmarkspritze
spine Rücken; Buchrücken
to splatter bespritzen
sprawling: to fall (fell – fallen) sprawling der Länge nach hinfallen
to spray wuchern, sprühen
spur-of-the-moment spontan
stab of fear plötzliche Angst
to stab stechen
stacks Bücherregale
staff Personal
staff HQ Stab
staggering umwerfend
to stain beflecken
to stake one's life on something auf etw. Gift nehmen
stale altmodisch

to stammer stottern
to stamp prägen
to stamp down on heftig treten auf
to stand (stood – stood) by someone jmdm. beistehen
starry sternenklar
to start back towards zugehen auf
to startle aufschrecken
stat sofort
state of mind Haltung, geistige Einstellung
to state angeben
to stay away nicht mehr kommen
to stay off one's feet sitzen oder liegen
steadily ruhig
steady stetig; sicher; beständig
steam Dampf
steam-driven dampfbetrieben
stench Gestank
to step into betreten
to step up kommen
sterling fabelhaft
stiffnecked starrsinnig
stillborn totgeboren
sting: to lose (lost – lost) its sting seinen Stachel verlieren
stocks Börsenberichte
stonily starr
stony felsig
stout unüberwindlich
to straighten glätten
straightforward direkt
strain Anstrengung
straining gespannt
to strap schnüren
streaked: to be (was/were – been) streaked with gore blutverschmiert sein
streaming tränend
strenuous anstrengend; ausdrücklich
stretch: not by any stretch of the imagination beim besten Willen nicht
stretcher Trage
strew of matchwood verstreutes Kleinholz
to strip off sich ausziehen
stripe Ärmelstreifen
to strobe erleuchten
strumpet Dirne
stub Abschnitt
stuffy steif
stunning atemberaubend
stutter Geknatter
sty Schweinestall
subconscious Unterbewusstsein
to subscribe to glauben an
subsequently später
to subside aufgeben
substitute Ersatz
to subvert untergraben
subway car U-Bahn-Wagen
succulent saftig
suffice to say … es reicht wohl, wenn ich sage …
suffocating erstickend
suited: to be (was/were – been) uniquely suited to wie geschaffen sein für
super Hausmeister(in)
superstitious abergläubisch
supervisor Vorgesetzte(r)
surge Woge
suspicion Misstrauen
sustained groß
susurrus Säuseln
to swear (swore – sworn) schwören

swirl: in a swirl wirbelnd
to swirl wirbeln
to switch to übergehen zu
to swoon in Ohnmacht fallen
syllable Silbe

T

to take (took – taken): it takes one to know one nur ein Dieb kennt einen Dieb
to take on annehmen
to take up durchführen
to take somebody up on something von etw. Gebrauch machen
to take up smoking zu rauchen anfangen
tale of unease unheimliche Geschichte
to talk somebody out of something jmdm. etw. ausreden
talkies Tonfilme
to tap klopfen
tattooed tätowiert
telling: it needs no telling man braucht es nicht zu erzählen
temple Schläfe
temptation Versuchung
to tend a bar Barkeeper sein
to tender geben
tenebrous dunkel
tentative unsicher
term: in the vaguest of terms äußerst vage
testicles Hoden
textured texturiert
Theater Society Theaterverein
thesis Behauptung
thin: to wear (wore – worn) thin langweilig werden
to thin: … had thinned to ribbons … kam jetzt nur in dünnen Fetzen
third finger Ringfinger
threatening drohend
three-piece-suited im Dreiteiler
threshold: to cross the threshold über die Schwelle treten
thrifty sparsam
throttle: to hold (held – held) the throttle of something etw. bestimmen
to thrust out hinausstoßen
thud dumpfer Schlag
thus so
to tick off tanzen auf
tie-clasp Krawattennadel
to tighten zusammenpressen
to tighten down sich straffen
time: in time nach und nach
time: the time has come die Zeit ist reif
timeless endlos
timid ängstlich
tinctured gestreckt
tinsel aus Rauschgold
tip Trinkgeld
tipsy beschwipst
tiptoe: to stand (stood – stood) on tiptoe sich auf die Zehenspitzen stellen
to tire oneself out sich erschöpfen
tiresome lästig
tissue-paper Seidenpapier
toast Trinkspruch
toe-scuffing zögernd
tom Truthahn
tome Wälzer
tongue-in-cheek ironisch
top: it's right up there in the top

ten es gehört zu den zehn merkwürdigsten
top: to be (was/were – been) on top of something etw. beherrschen
Top of the season! Schöne Feiertage!
topcoat Überzieher
top drawer Spitzenklasse
tophat Zylinderhut
to toss schieben
to tot up zusammenzählen
to total zusammenzählen
to totter torkeln
to towel sich abtrocknen
track Spur
traction Haftung
trademark Markenzeichen
trancelike wie in Trance
tranquil ruhig
transition Verwandlung
to trickle tröpfeln
trifle kleines bisschen
trimester Drittel
trip Besuch
trollop Hure
tropics Tropen
trove Fundgrube
truck-driver Lastwagenfahrer(in)
to trudge off lostrotten
trunk Kofferraum
to tuck schieben
to turn back zurückschlagen
to turn out: to be (was/were – been) turned out in something etw. tragen
to turn out sich als … erweisen
to turn something over to someone etw. an jmdm. weitergeben
turnout Teilnehmerzahl
turtlelike schildkrötenartig
tuxedo Smoking
twisted verbogen
to twitch zucken
twofold doppelt
typescript Manuskript

U

unasked unaufgefordert
uncanny: the uncanny das Übernatürliche
uncarpeted teppichlos
uncharted unbekannt
to unconvince verunsichern
to underestimate unterschätzen
undignified würdelos
unease Unbehagen
uneasily unsicher
unenviable nicht beneidenswert
unilluminating wenig informativ
unmarked unbedruckt
unmistakable unverkennbar
unnoticed unbemerkt
unobtrusively unauffällig, unaufdringlich
unpleasant unangenehm
unselfconsciousness Unbefangenheit
unspeakable unbeschreiblich
unstated unbewiesen
untinged with frei von
uproariously lärmend
uprooted aus dem Boden gerissen
to upset (upset – upset) beleidigen
uptown zu den besseren Kreisen
urge Drang
urge: to feel (felt – felt) an urge to do something das Bedürfnis verspüren, etw. zu tun
useless hilflos
to utilize anwenden

to utter ausstoßen
utterly völlig

V

to venture out sich hinaustrauen
verge: to be (was/were – been) on the verge of doing something im Begriff sein, etw. zu tun
verisimilitude Wahrhaftigkeit
very: that very thing genau das
vested persönlich
viciously verteufelt
view: she left my view ich verlor sie aus den Augen
vital lebenswichtig
vocal chords Stimmbänder
voluminous wallend
to vomit sich übergeben
vulnerable gefährdet

W

to wail wimmern
to wait on bedienen
to walk somebody to the door jmd. zur Tür bringen
warren Labyrinth
to wash fluten
washout Versager(in)
way: across the way gegenüber
way: to go (went – gone) out of one's way sich besondere Mühe machen
way: either way so oder so
way: my way mir zu
wayside: to fall (fell – fallen) by the wayside begraben werden
to wax and wane in der Lautstärke schwanken
wearily resigniert
to weave schwanken
wedding-band Ehering
wedlock: out of wedlock unverheiratet
weekly (Wochen-)Zeitung
to weep (wept – wept) weinen
welfare Sozialhilfe
well-bred wohlerzogen
well-equipped gut ausgerüstet
well off reich
whisk-broom Handfeger
whistle Pfeifen
whole im Ganzen
to whomp up erfinden
whoop Heulen
whorl Wirbel
to widen: her eyes widened sie machte große Augen
willful vorsätzlich
windpipe Luftröhre
wino Popsicle gefrorene Schnapsleiche
wisenheimer Besserwisser(in)
wistful wehmütig
wit: to survive on one's wits sich schlau durchs Leben schlagen
womb Gebärmutter
to work through somebody jmd. überkommen
Wot? (What?) Was?
to wrap einwickeln
to wrinkle one's nose die Nase rümpfen
to write (wrote – written) ausschreiben

Y

to yank open aufreißen
to yank up hochschlagen
Yellow gelbes Taxi
yet: as yet unexplored noch unbekannt